OSPREY AIRCRAFT OF THE ACES® • 47

SPAD XII/XIII
Aces of World War 1

SERIES EDITOR: TONY HOLMES

OSPREY AIRCRAFT OF THE ACES® • 47

SPAD XII/XIII
Aces of World War 1

Jon Guttman

OSPREY
PUBLISHING

Adjutant Pierre Gaudermen (far right) of SPA68 surveys his early-model SPAD XIII after a rough landing on frozen, broken ground at Toul in January 1918 – damage was limited to a broken propeller. Flying often with American squadronmate Reginald Sinclaire, Gaudermen was SPA68's only ace with five victories

Capitaine Georges Guynemer's SPAD XII S382 as it looked at the end of July 1917, with a dark (probably red) number '2,' a diagonal white fuselage band and the legend *VIEUX CHARLES* immediately below the exhaust pipe. On 27 and 28 July the ace used this cannon SPAD to add two victories to his score, and in spite of some teething troubles, he was pleased with the new fighter's potential (*via Leslie A Rogers*)

expectations, reaching a speed of 140 mph at 15,000 ft, and climbing to that altitude in 16 minutes and 18 seconds. On 9 June B3479 was sent to No 19 Sqn for frontline evaluation and four days later Capt Frederick Sowry drove down a German two-seater for his third victory. Lt G S Buck destroyed an Albatros the next day, and Fred Sowry became an ace in B3479 on 21 July, when he drove an Albatros D III down out of control north-east of Ypres. It would seem, then, that the British may actually have drawn first blood in the SPAD XIII, before its French creators. Soon, however, they would experience the same teething troubles with the geared Hispano-Suiza engine that were delaying the SPAD XIII's combat debut in the French *escadrilles*.

A CANNON-ARMED FIGHTER MADE FOR ACES

Another suggestion that Guynemer had made to Béchereau at the end of 1916 was for a fighter capable of mounting a cannon. By developing a variant on his geared engine (the 220-hp Hispano-Suiza 8Cb, which raised the propeller above the cylinder heads), Birkigt was indeed able to arrange a 37mm Puteaux cannon with a shortened barrel to fire through a hollow propeller shaft. Taking matters from there, Bechereau designed an enlarged version of the SPAD VII, which was designated the XIICa.1 (for type XII, cannon-armed single-seater).

In spite of its unusual armament, the SPAD XII did not look like a freak – in fact, with its lack of bulged fairings on the cockpit and slightly forward-staggered wings, it was one of the most elegant-looking SPADs ever built. Inside the cockpit, however, the cannon breech protruded between the pilot's legs, necessitating Deperdussin-type elevator and aileron controls on either side of the pilot, instead of a central control column.

When Capitaine Guynemer flew the SPAD XII in the spring of 1917, he recorded a maximum speed of 137 mph at ground level and a maximum ceiling of 23,000 ft. The main shortcoming that Guynemer saw in what he called his 'avion magique' was the fact that the 37mm cannon was a single-shot weapon, but the SPAD XII also had a single synchronised 0.303-in Vickers machine gun, which could be used to help sight the cannon on a target before the weapon was actually fired – or to help the pilot fight his way out of trouble after the cannon had been fired.

Guynemer in the cockpit of S382 in early September 1917, after it had undergone repairs. The replacement radiator cowl featured cooling holes and the fuselage was covered with new fabric. In its newly repainted form, it bore only SPA3's stork insignia, without any additional personal markings
(*Musée de l'Air et l'Espace via the author*)

SPAD XII S382 arrived at SPA3's aerodrome at St Pol-sur-Mer in July 1917, and during its first operational sortie on the 5th, Guynemer attacked a DFW C V whose gunner managed to inflict such damage that he had to turn his fighter in for repairs, which kept it grounded until the 20th. On 27 July, however, Guynemer used S382 to shoot down an Albatros scout between Langemarck and Roulers with eight machine-gun rounds and one cannon shell, killing Leutnant der Reserve Fritz Vossen of *Jagdstaffel* (or *Jasta*) 33. He downed a DFW C V over Westroosebeke the next day using two shells and 30 bullets, but his victim's return fire forced him to send S382 back to the repair shop until 15 August.

Guynemer scored a double victory on 17 August – one German two-seater with machine-gun fire alone, and a second with the cannon – but an inconclusive fight with an aggressive crew from yet another two-seater the very next day put his SPAD XII temporarily out of action once more.

In spite of the cannon fighter's mixed fortunes, Guynemer's performance encouraged the *Aviation Militaire* to send SPAD a contract for 1000 aircraft, but it is doubtful that more than 20 were completed before production problems with the engine and cannon arrangement led to the order being cancelled in favor of placing full priority on mass-producing the simpler SPAD XIII.

Successful though it had been in Guynemer's skilled hands, the SPAD XII was a handful for the average pilot. Aiming the cannon while using the Deperdussin controls required considerable dexterity. The weapon had a heavy recoil, fumes filled the cockpit after each firing, and reloading it by hand was easier said than done in the heat of combat, giving SPAD XII pilots reason to be grateful that they had a machine gun to fall back upon. On top of the cannon's problems, the geared Hispano-Suiza engine proved to be as troublesome in the SPAD XII as it did in the early XIIIs. In consequence, allocation of the cannon SPAD was generally limited to one or two per squadron, usually to a pilot of proven ability.

At least five SPAD XIIs besides Guynemer's bore variations on the famous stork emblem of *Groupe de Combat* (GC) 12, starting with the aircraft assigned to Capitaine Albert Deullin of SPA73. At least one other SPAD XII bore the *'cigogne au style japonais'* of SPA73, along with the red number 11 of Corsican ace Lt François Battesti, who professed to be quite pleased with the scout, and claimed at least one victory in it (probably his seventh, and last, on 28 October 1918). SPA3 received another SPAD XII sometime in 1918, which was probably flown by Georges Raymond (six victories) or Benjamin Bozon-Verduraz (eleven victories).

Two SPAD XIIs (S445 and S452) were flown by Sous-Lt René Paul Fonck of SPA103 during the spring of 1918. If ever man and machine were made for each other, Fonck and the cannon SPAD were, for he was a consummate pilot, marksman and tactician. And yet Fonck's first combat in the fighter was almost his last.

In his memoirs, Fonck described a fight with five German aircraft over Montdidier on 19 May 1918. Attacking from above, he sent 20 machine gun bullets into the rearmost enemy aeroplane, which nosed down into a spiralling dive. He also used the machine-gun to deal with a second adversary.

'For his part, my buddy (Sgt Jean) Brugére brought down another one', Fonck wrote, 'but (Sous-Lt Léon) Thouzellier, having engine

trouble, was at grips with the last two, who furiously tailed him and riddled him with bullets in his descent. Seeing him in such a bad spot, I tried to relieve him by a rapid turn, but as I was flying upside down, my extra cartridges, placed at my side in a case, fell among the controls and one of them got wedged'.

'I felt myself tearing through the air on my back at full speed', Fonck continued, 'and I was afraid at any instant that I would be shot down by the German whom I was about to attack, and who, realising my critical situation, would follow me firing away with his machine gun. I was carrying a new SPAD test gun for the first time, and I also did not know how to manoeuvre in order to get out of the situation Believing my situation to be hopeless, I resolved to risk everything. I abandoned the controls and picked up the scattered shells, which I threw over the side one by one. The few seconds this operation took seemed like an eternity to me, but I was finally able to straighten out 1000 m below. Never before did I feel death pass by so closely'.

One of the two two-seaters claimed by Fonck in that fight probably resulted in the deaths of Unteroffizier Walter Graf and Sgt Christian

Lt René Fonck poses beside one of two SPAD XIIs delivered to SPA103 in the spring of 1918. The serial number S452 can be made out on the left wheel hub
(*Musée de l'Air et l'Espace via Jon Guttman*)

Fonck climbs aboard his other SPAD XII, S445, which was fully marked with SPA103's stork emblem, the older red star insignia on the right upper wing and the ace's Roman numeral 'VI' on the fuselage sides and upper left wing

The two best pilots in SPA112 were Sgts Fernand Chavannes and Lionel de Marmier, who consequently shared the SPAD XII allotted to their *escadrille*. Signifying its joint 'ownership', the fighter featured the aces' intertwining initials on the fuselage side
(*SHAA B77.1623 via Jon Guttman*)

Höfele near Montdidier, while Brugére was credited with one of the fighter escorts. Fonck eventually claimed 11 of his victories in the SPAD XII, of which seven were confirmed.

SPA12 was issued a SPAD XII that was marked with the intertwined letters C and M, representing the two aces who shared it – Sgts Fernand Chavannes (seven victories) and Lionel de Marmier (six). Lt Armand de Turenne, 15-victory ace and commander of SPA12, was unimpressed

with his SPAD XII, stating that its cannon was inaccurate and 'the first time I used it, it threw my motor out of order'. Also less than enthused was Lt Henri Hay de Slade (19 victories), commander of SPA159. An American volunteer in his unit, Edwin B Fairchild, recalled;

'I had the chance to fly the cannon SPAD at Plessis-Belleville, but was too tall to fit in the cockpit. Slade got one, but he cracked it up – he also got behind a bomber, let fly, and it disappeared.'

Sgts Fernand Henri Chavannes and Lionel Alexandre Pierre de Marmier strike a comradely pose beside a SPAD VII of SPA112. The two friends teamed up in four of their victories, Chavannes' total amounting to seven, while de Marmier added two or three German aircraft to his six World War 1 victories while flying Caudron R 714s alongside Polish pilots in GC I/145 *'Varsovie'* in June 1940

SPAD XII S444 was marked with SPA15's insignia (the helmet of le Chevalier Bayard), the number '4' and a blue, white and red fuselage band. It was undoubtedly flown by one of that squadron's aces, probably Sous-Lt Gabriel Guérin, who scored 22 victories before being wounded on 11 May 1918. Later assigned to SPA88, Guérin claimed one more victory on 19 July before he was killed in a crash on 1 August

11

SPAD S444 bore the plumed knight's helmet insignia of SPA15 *'Chevalier Bayard'*, and may have been flown by that squadron's leading light in the spring of 1918, Lt Gabriel Guérin (23 victories). Lt Georges Félix Madon of SPA38 (41 victories) was allocated S434 and painted its fuselage and tail surfaces red, as he did with his SPAD XIIIs. Other cannon SPADs were flown by Lts Charles Nungesser of SPA65 (France's third-ranking ace with 43 victories) and Marcel Hugues (12 kills), commander of SPA95.

Two SPAD XIIs also went to France's allies. S449 was delivered to the RFC on 18 March 1918 and given the serial number B6877. Tested at Martlesham Heath, the machine was described by one pilot as being a 'soggy, nose-heavy job.' It crashed while being flown to the Isle of Grain on 4 April and was not rebuilt, nor did the British bother evaluating another.

The other SPAD XII went to the United States Army Air Service (USAS) in July 1918, and was originally intended for 1Lt David E Putnam of the 139th Aero Squadron, but he had yet to fly it operationally when he was killed in action on 12 September. The aeroplane was subsequently passed on to Capt Charles J Biddle, commander of the 13th Aero Squadron, who described it in a letter home on 8 October;

'The machine I mention is the only one of its kind in the American service, so I am very anxious to try it out. They gave it to me when Putnam was killed. Guynemer had one and Fonck and Deullin each have one, and have used them with fair success. I do not mean by this statement to be trying to class myself with them, so don't start to kid me on that score.

'This special gun is difficult to use, but if a shot ever hits a Hun he might just as well say his prayers and give up, if he has time to think about anything at all. I have my regular machine in addition, and we have really been so busy that I have not had time to try out the new one. It handles differently from our ordinary machines, and I wish to get considerable practice before I go monkeying around any Huns with it, for I should hate to be knocked out by some "Heinie" just because I could not manoeuvre my new aeroplane quickly.'

As a result of his cautious approach, Biddle probably never flew the cannon SPAD in combat before the war ended, scoring his eighth and final victory while flying his regular SPAD XIII on 18 October 1918.

Lt Marcel Anatole Hugues, commander of SPA95, stands beside his SPAD XII in May 1918. Born in Belfort on 5 January 1892, Hugues began his flying career as an observer in MF22, then trained to be a pilot. He went on to score his first victory with N77 on 14 February 1917, followed by two with N97, seven with SPA81 and his last two after being given command of SPA95 on 7 March 1918 (*Service Historique de l'Armée de l'Air B88.3588 via the author*)

The sole SPAD XII delivered to the USAS was originally slated for use by 1Lt David E Putnam, but after his death it was assigned to Capt Charles J Biddle, commander of the 13th Aero Squadron. It is shown here undergoing ground testing in October 1918. Biddle was unwilling to use his SPAD XII operationally until he had mastered its peculiar flying characteristics, and Germany signed the armistice before it saw any combat (*via Lafayette Foundation*)

Conceptually ahead of its time, the SPAD XII can hardly be regarded as a glorious success, but the principle it pioneered would later come to deadly fruition with the introduction of rapid-fire cannon. The few that saw action were flown by a large percentage of aces, but therein lay the problem – the SPAD XII had been built at the suggestion of an exceptional pilot and, as things turned out, only exceptional pilots could use it.

'STORKS' IN BATTLE

While Guynemer was waiting for his cannon fighter to be repaired, he received one of the earliest production SPAD XIIIs, S504, which he used to shoot down a DFW C V over Poperinghe on 20 August 1917. The first victory by a French SPAD XIII was also Guynemer's 53rd – and last. On the 24th, he visited the SPAD factory at Buc to inspect the repairs to his SPAD XII, and to recommend further improvements. Typically for Guynemer, who seldom rested, he was in a dangerously nervous state, and on the 28th he commented to a friend, 'I shall not survive'.

After returning to St Pol-sur-Mer, Guynemer was frustrated by bad weather on 8 and 9 September. He took off in S504 on the 10th, but had to land at a Belgian airfield when the aeroplane's water pump control became stuck. Guynemer returned to SPA3, borrowed Lt Deullin's SPAD, and attacked a large number of German aircraft, only to be struck by four bullets and compelled to land with a disabled air pump. Returning by automobile, Guynemer took off in another SPAD, but this time the fuel overflowed due to a loose carburetor cover and the engine caught fire, again forcing him to land.

Visibly exasperated, Guynemer ordered his mechanics to have S504 ready to fly at 0800 hrs the next morning, but fog delayed take-off until 0825 hrs on 11 September. Sous-Lt Bozon-Verduraz and Sgt Louis Risacher were slated to accompany him, but the latter's engine would not start and Guynemer impatiently took off with Bozon-Verduraz only.

At an altitude of 5000 ft the morning haze dissipated, and at 12,000 ft the Frenchmen spotted a DFW C V north-east of Ypres, which they attacked from above and behind. Bozon-Verduraz missed, and had pulled up to prepare for another diving pass when he noticed eight enemy aircraft approaching and turned toward them. The Germans turned away, so Bozon-Verduraz went back to find Guynemer, but could find no trace of either him or the DFW. Upon returning to St Pol-sur-Mer at 1020 hrs, Bozon-Verduraz's first words were, 'Has he landed yet?'

Guynemer had not, and a month later, the Germans announced that Leutnant Kurt Wissemann of *Jasta* 3 had killed the great ace for his fifth victory. Wissemann himself was not available for comment by then, having been killed on 28 September by two SE 5as of No 56 Sqn RFC, flown by Capt Geoffrey H Bowman and Lt R T C Hoidge. A sergeant of the German 413th Regiment certified that he had witnessed the SPAD's crash and identified the body, noting that Guynemer had died of a head wound, that one of his fingers had been shot off and a leg was broken. An Allied artillery barrage drove the Germans back before they could bury the body, which vanished amid the chaos that was the Western Front.

Whatever the tragic circumstances of his death, Georges Guynemer went into French legend as its second ranking ace who, a popular myth insisted, had flown so high he could never come down.

This classic photograph of Guynemer, taken while he was refitting the coolant pump on his SPAD XIII S504 at the Belgian aerodrome at Les Moëres on 10 September 1917, reveals the face of a man who has driven himself to the edge of his endurance. He failed to return from a patrol the following day (*via Greg VanWyngarden*)

SPAD XIIIs continued to make their way into GC12 and other squadrons over the next several months. In spite of its chronic engine troubles and its inferior manoeuvrabilty compared to the SPAD VII (especially in its early form, with the rounded wingtips), the XIII had the ability to lose most pursuers in a dive not only because of its speed, but because of the wing cellule's ability to hold up to the stress. The tactics devised to make the most of the SPAD XIII's strengths and minimise its weaknesses – similar to those employed by American pilots to outfight more nimble Japanese aircraft during World War 2 – were described by Charles Biddle in a letter home on 23 November 1917;

'You may think it sounds foolish, or as if one was blowing a bit of talk about, attacking five when we were only two, but an attack does not necessarily mean that you charge into the middle of them and mix it up. On the contrary, you can, by diving at high speed from above, get in some shots, and then by using your great speed climb up above them again out of reach before they get in a shot.

'If you remember to leave your motor on as you are diving, and in this way come down as fast as possible, without at the same time going so fast as to interfere with your shooting, the great speed gained in this way will enable you to make a short steep climb, and thus regain a position perhaps 200 metres above the heads of the Huns where they cannot effectively shoot at you. I am now of course speaking only of an attack on a group of single-seater machines.

'If the engagement ends here, the chances of bringing one down are not great, but you can sometimes by such methods, and by, for instance, hitting some part of one of the machines, so worry the Huns that one will in the general confusion get separated from his comrades so that you can get a fair crack at him.'

Born in Andalusia, Pennsylvania, on 13 May 1890, Biddle had graduated from Princeton University in 1911 and from Harvard in 1914, before being admitted to the Pennsylvania Bar in Philadelphia. Volunteering for French service through the *Lafayette* Flying Corps (LFC) on 8 April 1917, Biddle joined SPA73 on 28 July and learned much about aerial combat from its commander, Albert Deullin.

In contrast to the high-spirited young Americans who predominated in the LFC, Biddle tempered his patriotism with a maturity that facilitated his ability to learn the tactics necessary to survive in combat. On 7 November 1917, he received both a transfer and a promotion from a sergeant in the *Aviation Militaire* to a captain in the USAS, although he remained with SPA73 until 10 January 1918.

After indecisive encounters while flying the SPAD VII, Biddle obtained his first confirmed victory flying a XIII on 5 December 1917. He had noticed an Albatros two-seater crossing the lines at an altitude of about 4700 metres, and he flew underneath it from the opposite direction, then turned and approached from behind.

'All the time the Boche had not fired a shot, and from the way he acted I think he must have lost track of me behind his tail', Biddle wrote. 'Anyhow, I turned both my machine guns loose and thought I saw my bullets going about right. My left hand gun only fired about a dozen shots and then broke, the Boche at the same time giving a twist to the right to get me out from under his tail. I kept on plugging away with my other gun, shooting

Lt Benjamin Bozon-Verduraz was one of the SPA3 aces who came into his own in 1918. Adjutant André Martenot de Cordoux, who knew Bozon-Verduraz when the latter commanded SPA94, remembered him as a poor flyer and a poor shot, whose technique was simply to rush at his opponents, ignoring the return fire, until he could shoot them down at point-blank range!

Sgt Frank Leaman Baylies, a
***Lafayette* Flying Corps (LFC)**
volunteer from New Bedford,
Massachusetts, became SPA3's top
scorer of 1918 with 12 victories
(*via Greg VanWyngarden*)

for the place where the pilot sits, and again I thought I saw the bullets going into the right spot. After possibly 30 shots, however, my right gun also broke, leaving me with nothing, and at the same time the Hun started to join in the shooting, firing perhaps 20 shots.'

Biddle dived under the Albatros's tail, and as he looked back he saw it nose over and turn toward French lines upside down – 'a sign that all is not well on board, and it usually means that the pilot has fallen forward over the control stick,' he remarked. He followed it down from 4000 to 1000 m, alternately squeezing off shots until he found both guns 'not simply jammed but broken'.

'A quick, great change of altitude like this is most unpleasant', he added, 'as your ears get all stopped up and it gives you a headache, but in a fighter you do not at the time notice it, and this time I was very anxious to see where the Boche fell so as to get him confirmed if he did go down'. Biddle was finally rewarded by the sight of the Albatros on its back near Langmarck. The crew, Leutnants Fritz Pauly and Ernst Sauter of *Flieger Abteilung* 45, were killed.

Another early American to fly the SPAD XIII in SPA73 was Cpl Frank Leaman Baylies. Born in New Bedford, Massachusetts, on 23 September 1895, Baylies had volunteered for the ambulance service in May 1916, serving at the Somme, Verdun and in Serbia, before joining the LFC. He arrived at SPA73 on 17 November 1917 and, as the *escadrille*'s 13th member, he was assigned aircraft No 13. 'Cannot afford to be superstitious – nothing like being a fatalist', Baylies wrote in a letter home.

In January 1918 SPA73 was detached from GC12 and combined with SPA85, 95 and 96 to form GC19. Capitaine Deullin was promoted to command the groupe, and on 19 May he shot down an Albatros east of Montdidier for his 20th, and last, victory. Deullin survived the war, but was killed on 29 May 1923 while testing a prototype aeroplane at Villacoublay.

Back at GC12, SPA3's pilots tried to revive the glory of the Guynemer era, and its leading ace in 1918 was American Frank Baylies, who had transferred to the original *'Escadrille des Cigognes'* from SPA73 on 18 December 1917. After a quiet winter, Cpl Baylies opened his account by downing a two-seater over French lines on 19 February 1918. 'It was mighty exciting – much better than duck shooting and much more profitable', he wrote home.

Lt Georges Raymond, who had assumed command of SPA3 on 2 November 1917, joined the ranks of the 'Stork' aces on 20 February by adding an enemy aeroplane to the four he had downed earlier while flying SPAD VIIs. On 16 March the recently promoted Sgt Baylies attacked three German fighters and sent one spinning down to crash.

On the 28th, however, Baylies lost a fight with a two-seater in what he called 'a real dime novel affair'. Force-landing between the lines, he took the time to remove the watch and altimeter from his wrecked SPAD before sprinting to French lines, pursued by a detachment of German troops, three of whom were shot by the French before he made it to the safety of their trenches.

Baylies sent an artillery spotting aeroplane down in flames on 11 April, and scored his fourth victory the next day. On 24 April, Adjutant Edwin Charles Parsons joined SPA3. Born in Holyoke, Massachusetts, on

24 September 1892, Parsons had learned to fly in 1912, and had briefly taken up an offer from Mexican revolutionary Francisco 'Pancho' Villa to train airmen, but made a hasty exit after he learned of Villa's raid on Columbus, New Mexico. Later serving in the famed *escadrille* N124 *'Lafayette'*, Parsons downed a Rumpler on 4 September 1917, and chose to remain with the French when his unit was transferred to the USAS in February 1918.

On 2 May Baylies was returning from a patrol in a SPAD XIII 'borrowed' from Bozon-Verduraz when he spotted three Rumplers overhead. Baylies stood the SPAD on its tail and, in his own words, 'let Mr Hun have the benefit of two perfectly-working, well-regulated machine guns. He didn't have much to say and fell out of control, hit the ground with an awful blow, and lay there a crumpled mass of debris'.

Now an ace, Baylies assisted a future ace on 3 May when he and Maréchal-des-Logis (MdL) André Dubonnet, 20-year-old scion of the Parisian wine-producing family, shot a two-seater down in flames over Montdidier, killing Leutnants Willi Karbe and Erich Meuche of *Flieger Abteilung* (*Fl Abt*) 245. On 6 May Parsons, whose usual SPAD XIII bore the number '4', opened his account at SPA3 by downing a two-seater.

SPA3 was not the only 'Stork' *escadrille* striving to uphold GC12's notoriety. On 25 December 1917, SPA26 got a new commander for Christmas in the person of Lt Joseph Marie Xavier de Sevin. Born in Toulouse on 10 March 1894, de Sevin was attending the military academy at St-Cyr when war broke out, and he volunteered for infantry service on 2 September 1914. On 15 July 1915, he transferred to Pau for flight training, joined N12 on 11 November, and shot down six enemy aeroplanes with that unit between 11 July 1917 and 30 September 1917. De Sevin gained his first victory with SPA26 on 20 January 1918, and scored again on 1 April.

The top-scoring pilot in GC12 was Sous-Lt René Fonck of SPA103, whose stalking tactics combined perfectly with the SPAD XIII's characteristics to raise his score from 20 to 36 between 19 January and 22 April.

Fonck's self-absorbed attitude alienated his fellow Storks, however, and during one of his pompous lectures on how to be a successful fighter pilot, Baylies and Parsons bet a bottle of champagne that they could shoot down a German before he could. Fonck accepted, and on 9 May, despite hazy conditions, Baylies caught a Halberstadt CL II between Braches and Gratibus, and sent it crashing behind German lines.

Back at the groupe's aerodrome at Hétomesnil, Fonck complained that bad weather had prevented him from going on patrol, and asked that the wager be altered to favour whoever downed the most enemy aeroplanes that day. Reluctantly, the Americans agreed.

Fonck did not fly until 1500 hrs, but an hour later he claimed three

Capitaine Joseph Marie Xavier de Sevin, commander of SPA26, poses with his SPAD XIII in the autumn of 1918. He used a personal motif – a rose in a hunting horn – to identify his aeroplane, rather than the more conventional number '1'. Promoted to capitaine on 24 June 1918, Xavier de Sevin survived the war with 12 victories two-seaters south of Moreuil that fell within 400 yards of each other, all in a matter of 45 seconds. Baylies and Parsons set out again at 1730 hrs, but had no further luck. At the same time, Fonck was patrolling with Thouzelier and Brugére, but lost them in some fog. Upon emerging from it, he spotted a German two-seater over Montdidier, which he shot down.

Fonck admitted that he was pleased to have lost his wingmen, stating 'I prefer to fly alone in the middle of my adversaries anyway, without having the additional responsibilities of protecting my comrades.I try never to let a comrade down, but above all, I like my freedom of action, for it is indispensable to the success of my undertakings'.

At 1856 hrs Fonck encountered four Fokker D VIIs, with five Albatros scouts flying above them. 'I hesitated to attack', Fonck wrote, 'but the desire to round out my performance won out over prudence, and I chose the risks of combat'. Diving on the Fokkers, he picked off the trailing aeroplane, and in the next eight seconds manoeuvred into position to shoot down the leader, then dived away from the seven remaining fighters. His victims, Leutnant Ernst Schulze and Unteroffizier Otto Kutter of *Jasta* 48, were both killed. Fonck had won the champagne with a phenomenal total of six victories in one afternoon.

Baylies and MdL Georges Clément downed a two-seater on 10 May, while Dubonnet got another. Six Germans fell to GC12 pilots on 15 May, including a two-seater downed by Bozon-Verduraz and MdL Edouard Moulines of SPA3. Parsons, MdL Jean Denneulin and Sgt Maurice Chevannes claimed a two-seater the following day, as did Louis Risacher, a skilled pilot who had been with SPA3 since July 1917. He shared his kill with Bozon-Verduraz and Moulines. While Fonck scored his double victory in his SPAD XII on 19 May, Parsons also got one, and claimed his fifth kill on the 20th. Baylies shot down enemy aeroplanes on 28 and 29 May, and on the 31st he claimed his 12th victory in concert with Dubonnet. Bozon-Verduraz also scored on 29 May, and Dubonnet and Chevannes burned a balloon on 13 June.

On 17 June Baylies, 'borrowing' Risacher's SPAD because his own was giving him trouble, was leading Dubonnet and Sgt François Macari on patrol when they spotted a formation of four rotary-engined aeroplanes above them which they assumed to be British Sopwiths. Baylies was leading his wingmen to join them when Dubonnet reported that Baylies' SPAD 'leaped upward and then swung over on one wing' as he realised his error and three Fokker Dr Is dived on him. Baylies looped and managed to get on the tail of one of his attackers, but the fourth Fokker, which had held back for just such an eventuality, pounced on his SPAD and shot him down in flames near Rollot.

In the unequal combat that followed, Macari disengaged safely, but Dubonnet barely managed to crash-land in Allied lines. Baylies was probably the victim of Leutnant Rudolf Rienau of *Jasta* 19, while Dubonnet was credited to Leutnant Wilhelm Leusch. On 6 July a German aeroplane dropped the following message over French lines, 'Pilot Baylies killed in combat. Buried with military honours'. In 1927 his body was reinterred at the *Memorial de l'Escadrille Lafayette* in the Parc Revue Villeneuve l'Étang, eight miles outside of Paris.

Combat was not the only means by which SPA3 lost its best pilots. On 1 July Bozon-Verduraz left to take command of SPA94. Risacher, after

Sous-Lt Louis Risacher strikes a dashing pose beside his Blériot-built SPAD XIII in June 1918. He told the author that his red number '17' was applied over the camouflage, giving it a reddish brown appearance This may have been the machine that Baylies was flying when he was killed on 17 June

defeating a German fighter on 9 August, was transferred to SPA159 eight days later. Finally, Raymond, promoted to capitaine in May 1918, and later made a *Chevalier de la Légion d'Honneur*, had to relinquish command of SPA3 on 3 September when he came down with pneumonia – from which he died in hospital on 4 October.

Only two aces remained in SPA3 when the war ended. On 16 August Dubonnet shared in two successes – one with SPA103's commander, Capitaine Joseph Battle, the other with Capitaine de Sevin of SPA26 – to raise his total to six. Parsons downed a Fokker D VII on 26 August, teamed up with MdL Denneulin and Sous-Lt Pierre Pendaries of SPA67 to destroy a two-seater south of Tahure on 26 September, and scored his eighth victory (another two-seater) on 1 October. Dubonnet, who became a *Chevalier de la Légion d'Honneur* in January 1936, served in GCI/2 during World War 2, and died on 20 January 1980.

During the post-war years, Ed Parsons worked as an agent for the Federal Bureau of Investigation and as a writer or advisor on several aviation films. He also wrote for 'pulp' magazines, published a book on his wartime experiences and wrote and narrated a 15-minute radio series, 'Heroes of the *Lafayette*'. In 1940, Parsons joined the US Navy as a lieutenant commander, served in the Solomon Islands and had risen to the rank of rear admiral by the end of World War 2. After receiving a rather overdue *Légion d'Honneur* in 1962, Parsons died on 2 May 1968 and was buried in Arlington National Cemetery.

Among the other *escadrille*s of GC12, Adjutant Gustave Naudin of SPA26 gained his sixth victory on 31 July, but was wounded on 29 September, and Pierre Pendaries of SPA67 added four to the three earlier successes he had achieved while serving in N69. The group's outstanding squadron of 1918, however, was SPA103, whose wartime total of 111 ranked it second only to SPA3, with 175. Most remarkably, 73 of SPA103's victories had been scored by one man – René Fonck.

Of the *escadrille*'s other aces, Claude Marcel Haegelen had downed two enemy aeroplanes in 1917, scoring the rest of his 22 victories with SPA100, while Adjutant Auguste Baux allegedly downed five before being killed in action on 17 July 1918. Another member, Sous-Lt Louis Fernand Coudouret, had claimed two victories in 1916 – one with N57 and one with N102 – and three in 1917 while serving with N581 in Russia, before joining SPA103 on 18 May. His sixth, and last, came on 2 June 1918, when he and an LFC squadronmate, Sgt Robert B Hoeber, downed a German fighter over Carlepont.

Throughout the summer of 1918, Fonck's score grew steadily – often by two or three victories a day. Then, on 26 September, he left La Noblette aerodrome, north of Châlons, and encountered five Fokker D VIIs. 'Without giving them time to work out by signals their plan to attack me', he later wrote, 'I dived into their midst at full speed, guns blazing. Letting myself then fly on my wing, I turned over completely in order to rocket up behind one of the aeroplanes which had already fired at me. But I also had fired, and two of the German aeroplanes crashed to earth in the vicinity of Sommepy. The others, fearing for their safety, had thought it more prudent to take to their heels'.

Regaining height, Fonck noticed a Halberstadt two-seater coming under French anti-aircraft fire, and he attacked it over Perthes-les-Hurlus, killing its observer, Lt.d.R Eugen Anderer of *Fl Abt* (A) 233, with his first shots. 'The defenseless pilot became frightened,' Fonck reported, 'and his vertical dive was so sudden and steep that his companion, whom I had just sent off to join his ancestors, toppled overboard and almost fell on top of me at the moment of finishing my loop, when I was going to climb in order to attack the two-seater again'. Fonck then sent the enemy aeroplane crashing minus a wing, killing its pilot, Unteroffizier Richard Scholl.

Leading an evening patrol with three squadronmates, Fonck encountered eight more Fokkers. 'I awaited the attack confidently and would have willingly provoked it when a SPAD came in unexpectedly to lend a hand', Fonck said. 'I immediately recognised Capitaine de Sevin and the "Storks" of the 26th'.

The French attacked, but the Germans gave Fonck one of the most difficult fights of his career. Adjutant Brugére downed a Fokker, but was attacked by two others, one of which Fonck claimed to have shot down in the process of rescuing him. 'During this time', Fonck added, 'Capitaine de Sevin was going through a very risky acrobatic manoeuvre in order to shake off a Boche who had come to grips with him, and who seemed to me to be a rather bold devil. Only the captain's skill as a pilot permitted him to escape, for his motor had conked out and he was pursued to within 100 metres of the ground'.

Five Albatros two-seaters entered the melée, and Fonck downed two of them as well. 'Two others owed their skins to a jamming of my machine gun', he stated, 'and despite the cold, which perpetually reigns in high altitude, I must confess I felt drenched with perspiration upon returning to the field. But for me, the day had been excellent. I now had 66 official victories to my credit'.

Fonck had also scored his second sextuple victory. British Sopwith Camel aces John Trollope and Henry Woollett, and German Fokker D VII pilot Franz Büchner had equalled Fonck's feat, but only he had done it twice. One of Fonck's victories was also claimed by de Sevin, but credited to Fonck – who, by virtue of not having crash-landed, had been able to submit his claim first. De Sevin's SPAD, which came down behind French lines, was one of two credited to Leutnant der Reserve Karl

A former member of the famed *Lafayette Escadrille* N124, who stayed with the French in preference to transferring to the USAS, Sous-Lt Edwin Charles Parsons scored seven of his eight victories with SPA3

Lt Bernard Henri Barny de Romanet scored ten victories with SPA37, the last of which was on 22 August 1918 – the very day he was appointed to command the newly-formed SPA167. Under de Romanet's leadership, SPA167 was credited with ten victories in one month (eight of which were credited to the commander) without loss. Made a *Chevalier de la Légion d'Honneur*, de Romanet was killed in a flying accident on 23 September 1921

With one balloon and three enemy aeroplanes to his credit before being wounded on 23 May 1917, former N3 pilot Joseph-Henri Guiguet was assigned to SPA167 as a sous-lieutenant on 29 August 1918. Guiguet finally attained ace status on 24 October, when he and de Romanet downed a two-seater north of Attigny

Maletsky of *Jasta* 50, but one of the Germans, Visefeldwebel Karl Weinmann, also came down in French territory and was taken prisoner.

October saw GC12 credited with 31 enemy aeroplanes destroyed. Nearly a third of these were scored by 'Stork' squadron SPA167, which had been formed on 22 August 1918 under Lt Bernard Henri Barny de Romanet, who had previously downed ten opponents with SPA37, the last of these being claimed on the very day he was assigned to his new command.

SPA167 did not commence operations until late September, but under de Romanet's leadership, its pilots shot down ten enemy aeroplanes in a month without loss. Eight fell to the commander, including a two-seater downed north of Attigny in collaboration with Sous-Lt Joseph-Henri Guiguet on 24 October. A former member of N3, Guiguet had accounted for one balloon and three aeroplanes before being wounded on 23 May 1917 – sharing in de Romanet's 17th victory raised him to ace status at last. Xavier de Sevin also scored on the 24th, bringing his total to 12. Later serving in World War 2, he rose to the rank of Général de Division Aerienne (major general) and was made a *Grand Officier de la Légion d'Honneur*, dying on 7 November 1963. De Romanet was less fortunate, being killed in a flying accident on 23 September 1921.

October also saw the return to combat of one of France's great pre-war aviators, and pioneer fighter pilots, Lt Roland Garros. Using steel deflectors on the propeller of his modified Morane-Saulnier L parasol, Garros had scored three victories in April 1915, but came down behind German lines on the 18th and was taken prisoner. After several failed attempts, he finally escaped on 14 February 1918, and after rehabilitation and retraining, he was assigned to SPA103 on 20 August, transferring to SPA26 three days later.

Aggressive as ever, he claimed two Fokker D VIIs on 2 October, one of which was confirmed for his fourth victory, but his long-overdue ace status was not to be attained. On 5 October Garros went missing, his SPAD XIII S15409, bearing the number '30', having last been seen engaging seven Fokkers south-west of Vouziers. World War 1's first fighter pilot was probably killed by Lt.d.R. Hermann Habich of *Jasta* 49, who claimed a SPAD XIII near Sommepy.

Fonck shot down two enemy aeroplanes on 5 October, followed by three on the 30th and two on the 31st. His victory over a Halberstadt on 1 November was also the last for GC12, bringing its total to 286 aircraft and five ballooons destroyed, although if one counted their victories prior to the groupe's formation, the collective wartime total of its component *escadrilles* came to 411 aeroplanes and 11 balloons.

With 75 confirmed victories – and 52 unconfirmed – René Fonck was the undisputed Allied 'ace of aces', yet he never received the public adulation that went to Guynemer or Nungesser. In 1926 he tried to fly the Atlantic Ocean from New York to Paris, but his overloaded Sikorsky S 35 crashed on take-off, killing two of its four-man crew. Fonck served as inspector of France's fighter force prior to 1940, but after World War 2 he was accused of collaborating with the Germans, although he was never brought to trial. René Fonck was 59 when he died in Paris on 18 June 1953, an unrequited seeker of glory who could easily have stood on the record of his deeds – if only he had seen fit to do so.

SPAD XIIIs FOR THE ALLIES

British Aces

With the notable exception of the United States, the SPAD XIII saw much less wartime use by France's allies than the SPAD VII. Russia evaluated a SPAD XIII, but France's needs, combined with the turmoil of the Revolution, prevented the type from serving there in quantity. Belgium purchased 37 SPAD XIIIs and assigned them to the *10éme Escadrille* in March 1918, but the squadron's only ace, Edmond Thieffry, had been shot down and taken prisoner on 23 February 1918. The only Belgians to achieve acedom in 1918 were Willy Coppens and André Demeulemeester, and they did so flying Hanriot HD 1s. Italy and Britain used SPAD XIIIs in combat, but neither used many of them, and the latter did not use them for very long.

Following the creditable performance shown by SPAD XIII B3479 with No 19 Sqn in the summer of 1917, the RFC placed a contract for 130 SPAD XIIIs with Avionneries Kellner et ses Fils, but the first airframe (S4311) did not arrive at Villacoublay until nearly November – and the new owners could not get its engine started until the 10th! Subsequent deliveries were disrupted by a decree from French authorities that half of Kellner's output must go to the *Aviation Militaire*. Only 20 SPAD XIIIs had reached the RFC by 12 January 1918, and probably no more than 57 were delivered by April, at which time the newly reorganised Royal Air Force announced that no more were required.

The only British unit to be fully equipped with SPAD XIIIs was No 23 Sqn, which received its first aeroplanes in December 1917. By 1 February 1918, its inventory comprised 13 SPAD XIIIs and five 180-hp SPAD VIIs – one week later, it finally reached its full strength of 16 SPAD XIIIs. All had rounded wingtips, which the French retroactively offered to improve by sewing three-ply wooden 'pockets' on the ailerons and wingtips to produce a squarer profile, and thus improve lateral control. The British declined the offer after an advisory report from the RFC representative in the Ministry of Munitions Paris office stated, 'The execution of the work is badly carried out, and should the twine rot or fray, the three-ply corner would become detached, probably jamming or damaging the aileron.'

SPAD XIIIs of No 23 Sqn line up at La Lovie in early February 1918 (*via Leslie Rogers*)

Baracca poses beside his 34th and last victory, Oeffag Albatros D III 153.266, which he and Aliperta forced down at San Biagio di Callata on 15 June 1918. The injured pilot, Leutnant Sigismund von Josipovich of *Fliegerkompagnie* 51J, became an airline pilot in Austria after the war (*Embassy of Italy via Jon Guttman*)

injured, but recovered and became an airline pilot in Austria after the war.

At 0630 hrs on the morning of 19 June, Baracca and a new pilot, Tenente Franco Osnago, took off to support the infantry, but during their strafing attacks both Italians' SPADs were hit by ground fire and they became separated.

A few minutes later, Osnago observed an aeroplane spinning down in flames over Montello. Even from Baracca's aerodrome, witnesses saw an aeroplane falling 'like a meteor', but it caused little concern until the 91st's commander became overdue to land. Not until days later, after the Austro-Hungarians had retreated, was Baracca's body found, lying four metres from his burnt SPAD XIII near Buda della Rane, with a small black hole in the middle of his forehead.

Soon afterward, the Austro-Hungarian Nachrichtenblatt (information sheet) announced that a Phönix C I crew (Zugsführer Max Kauer and Oberleutnant Arnold Barwig) from *Flik* 28 had shot down Baracca. The Italians hotly denied the claim, insisting that 'The vaunt of bringing down Major Baracca belongs to an obscure Austrian infantryman who succeeded with his machine gun in shooting the heroic major down while he was flying very low and attacking enemy parties in movement on the foot bridges across the Piave'. Adding some plausibility to the Italian counterclaim was the fact that they had lost two other fighter pilots on 19 June, either of whom could just as likely have been the victims of Kauer and Barwig.

Whatever the cause, Baracca's death had a similar effect on the Italians as the loss of Georges Guynemer had on the French and Manfred von Richthofen's demise had on the Germans. Baracca's famed prancing horse became the insignia for the *4° Stormo* (wing) during World War 2, but no Italian pilot equalled his score of 34 victories during the latter conflict. The ace's cavallino rampante lives on still as the emblem of Enzo Ferrari's racing team (the badge also adorns the company's road cars).

After Baracca's death, command of *91ª Squadriglia* was given to Capitano Fulco Ruffo di Calabria, who had been awarded the *Medaglia d'Oro al Valore Militare* on 5 May, and had since downed three more enemy aeroplanes by 15 June, bringing his total to 20.

The war was catching up with Ruffo too, however, for soon after taking over the unit, he suffered a nervous breakdown and had to relinquish command to Tenente Ferruccio Ranza. Already an ace with more than 16 enemy aeroplanes to his credit as of 15 June, Ranza brought down a two-seater on 17 August, and added a further three 'probables' by the end of the war.

Promoted to capitano, Ranza was knighted in the Military Order of Savoy and also received three *Croci d'Argento al Valore Militare*, two *Croci di Bronzo*, four war crosses (two Italian, one French and one Belgian) and the Serbian Star of Karageorgevich. When he retired from an equally distinguished career in the Regia Aeronautica on 29 January 1945, Ranza was a generale di squadra aerea.

As with France's 'Storks' after Guynemer's death, newer members of *91ª Squadriglia* strove both to emulate and avenge Baracca. There were still some 'old hands' in the unit, such as Tenente Colonello Pier Piccio, who had 17 victories when he resumed his scoring in the SPAD XIII on 26 May 1918, and raised his total to 24 on 11 August to become the second-ranking Italian ace. His victories on those dates were shared with Tenente Novelli, bringing the latter pilot's tally to eight. Sergente Magistrini scored his sixth victory over an enemy fighter on 12 July.

Capitano Bartolomeo Constantini, who had scored his first four kills in SPAD VIIs between 25 October and 30 November 1917, used the SPAD XIII to down an Albatros D III over San Lucia di Piave on 12 August 1918, and to destroy a two-seater in flames over Marano di Piave on the 22nd, during which he reported seeing the observer parachute to safety.

In addition to the Italian *squadriglie*, a fighter unit attached to the French X. *Armée* in northern Italy, SPA561 *'l'Escadrille de Venise'*, began adding SPAD XIIIs to the Nieuports and SPAD VIIs in its inventory in 1918. At the end of the war the unit was credited with 12 enemy aircraft and four balloons destroyed.

Its sole ace, Sgt André Robert Lévy, was born in Paris on 6 June 1893, and he had served in the infantry before transferring to aviation on 8 October 1916. Lévy first flew Farmans in F29, but was flying a Sopwith 1.A2 when he shared the credit for downing an enemy aeroplane over Berry-au-Bac on 7 April 1917. He was assigned to N561 on 16 May, and on 16 November he and MdL Edmond Corniglion shot down an Austro-Hungarian floatplane. Lévy used a dog's head as his personal marking on the fuselages of his Nieuport and SPAD fighters, scoring victories in the latter aircraft on 21 June, 20 July and 5 August 1918.

On 16 September Lévy burned a balloon of *Ballonkompagnie* 3 west of Ceggia, but anti-aircraft fire from *Luftfahrzeug-Abwehrbatterie* 6/146 struck his SPAD XIII, severing the fuel line. With his engine dead, Lévy deliberately made a hard landing, buckling his undercarriage and flipping his aeroplane onto its back. After one failed attempt, Lévy succeeded in escaping from from Mulbach prison camp on 2 November. Traversing a 2500-metre mountain through two-and-a-half feet of snow on foot, he managed to reach the Italian border on 5 November and rejoined his *escadrille* at Lido on the 6th.

In addition to being made a *Chévalier de la Légion d'Honneur*, and receiving the *Médaille Militaire* and *Croix de Guerre* with two *Étoiles de bronze*, Sgt Lévy was awarded the Italian *Croce da Guerra*, two *Medaglie d'Oro* and two *Medaglie da Bronzo al Valore Militare*. Lévy died on 12 March 1973.

Capitano Fulco Ruffo di Calabria (centre, with the cap on) and his squadronmates stand beside his SPAD XIII which, like Baracca's, continued to sport his old death's head personal marking instead of the *91ª Squadriglia's* griffon emblem. At least three of his 20 victories were scored while flying the SPAD XIII (*via Roberto Gentilli*)

MAINSTAY OF THE CHASSE AERIENNE

As the war entered its final year, French *escadrilles de chasse* were still largely equipped with SPAD VIIs, powered by the 180-hp direct-drive Hispano-Suiza 8Ab engine. These remained in service while the teething troubles with the SPAD XIII's geared 8B engines were addressed and remedied. SPAD also tried to improve the lateral flying characteristics of early XIIs and XIIIs by sewing three-ply wooden pocket extensions over the rounded wingtips and ailerons, which in spite of their hazardous nature turned up as late as October 1918 on the lower wings of American 1Lt Arthur Raymond Brooks' SPAD XIII S7689 which survives at the National Air and Space Museum in Washington, DC. A more reliable solution lay in later production SPAD XIIIs, built with squared wingtips from the outset.

Gradually, SPAD XIIIs began to eclipse the VII until, by the late summer of 1918, *groupes de combat*, each comprising four or five *escadrilles*, were operating the new fighter in force from Flanders to Alsace-Lorraine.

Early versions of the SPAD XII and XIII were covered with yellow-doped fabric, with the forward fuselage, panels, undercarriage, fuel tanks and any other metal parts painted a glossy light yellow to roughly match that colour. In October 1917, production aircraft began to appear in five-colour camouflage, consisting of black, chestnut brown, beige and light and dark green, the paint being hand-brushed on the aircraft in accordance to a standardised pattern, although those patterns varied from one sub-contractor to another. Just how effective this camouflage pattern was in concealing SPADs on the ground, or flying at low altitude, remains open to debate – most pilots who flew them doubted its usefulness – but the paint, which with the exception of the lamp black, was mixed with aluminium powder, did serve to protect the canvas from the the elements.

Lt Armand Jean Galliot Joseph, Marquis de Turenne, of SPA12 stands beside his SPAD XIII – probably around 14 May 1918, when his unit was cited in General Orders for downing 34 enemy aircraft and two balloons since he took command on 12 January. Instead of applying the blue and white pennant of SPA12 to his aeroplane, Turenne preferred to keep the cockerel's head of his old unit, SPA48, as a personal marking (*Service Historique de l'Armée de l'Air B77.1090, via Jon Guttman*)

In January 1918 the French expanded further on the concept of the *groupe de combat*, or its German equivalent, the *Jagdgeschwader*, as a means of achieving local air superiority. *Escadre de Combat* 1, commanded by the veteran Chef de Bataillon Victor Menard, combined GC15 (SPA37, 81, 93 and 97), GC18 (SPA48, 94, 153 and 155) and GC19 (SPA73, 85, 95 and 96).

The *escadre de combat* concept, which gave the French a single unified command that could move 12 fighter units to whichever sector required their services, was soon put to the test. At 0440 hrs on the morning of 21 March 1918, the Germans commenced a general offensive that represented their final bid for victory over the Allied armies on the Western Front before the American Expeditionary Force (AEF) could arrive in sufficient strength to affect the war. It began with a concentrated bombardment by 6000 German guns against the British Third and Fifth Armies along the 42-mile-front south of Arras, which were then assaulted by the 2. *Armee* under Gen Georg von der Marwitz, the 17. *Armee* under Gen Karl von Bülow and the 18. *Armee* under Gen Oskar von Hutier.

The mastermind behind the German push, Gen Erich Ludendorff, ordered von Bulow's 17. *Armee* to seize the critical rail centre of Amiens, while Hutier was to direct his 18. *Armee* along the right flank of the reeling British Fifth Army, driving a wedge between it and the French army to the south. When the offensive finally stalled along the Somme River, the German 7., 18. and 1. *Armees* stormed southward along the Chemin des Dames on 28 May, smashing through Général Denis Duchéne's *VIéme Armée*, as well as the *Xéme and Véme Armées* in an attempt to force a direct route to Paris.

This final struggle for the initiative on the Western Front was accompanied by a relentless succession of aerial engagements over the contested ground. Ready or not, the SPAD XIII and its pilots were heavily committed, not only to seizing control the sky, but to the more hazardous business of ground attack missions against the advancing Germans, in the face of withering ground fire.

THE 1918 GENERATION

Numerous French aces who had started scoring in Nieuports and SPAD VIIs completed their tallies in SPAD XIIIs, but their introductions to the latter fighter varied widely, depending on when a given *escadrille* was re-equipped with it. Arguably the most radical transition was made by

This evocative photograph of SPA97 fighters shows a newly arrived SPAD XIII in the right foreground, while the rest of the machines are SPAD VIIs

29

Lt Charles Eugéne Jules Marie Nungesser, the freelancing ace of SPA65, who had scored most of his previous victories in Nieuport 17, 17bis and 25 scouts. He was probably flying a SPAD XIII when he downed two enemy two-seaters on 4 May 1918, and must have appreciated its speed and robust structure on 14 August when he burned four German kite balloons.

Twenty-four hours later, Charles Nungesser achieved his last confirmed success in a rare team effort with Adjutant Marcel Laurent Henriot and Sgt Millot. Nungesser's 43rd victory was also counted as the fifth for Henriot, who went on to score his sixth on 28 September.

Finally forsaking his Nieuports, Lt Charles Nungesser of SPA65 sits atop his SAFCA-built SPAD XIII, S10039, marked with his trademark Coeur Noir, an asymmetrical panel on the upper fuselage and the legend *LT VERDIER* below the cockpit, the latter marking being in reference to his deceased friend, Lt Louis Verdier-Fauvety. Also of interest is the early air-to-air camera on the upper wing (*SHAA B76.902 via Jon Guttman*)

Sous-Lt Georges Félix Madon was already one of France's greatest heroes of the air when he was put in command of his *escadrille*, SPA38, on 24 March 1918. Three years earlier, on 5 April 1915, he had landed his aeroplane in error in Switzerland and been interned, but he escaped on 27 December. Since then, Madon had been credited with 25 victories by 9 March 1918. Flying SPAD XIIs and XIIIs, usually with red-painted fuselages, he raised his official score to 41 on 3 September 1918 – he also had roughly 100 unconfirmed victories to his credit too.

As impressive as Madon's status as France's fourth-ranking ace, however, was the number of fighter pilots who credited him with helping them to perfect their own tactics, including André Martenot de Cordoux and David Putnam. Promoted to capitaine at the end of the war, and subsequently made an *Officier de la Légion d'Honneur*, Madon was tragically killed in a flying accident in Tunis on 11 November 1924 – ironically, while participating in an Armistice Day display that also marked the inauguration of a statue of Roland Garros.

Lt Georges Félix Madon (right) poses with an unidentified observer and a squadron mascot in the cockpit of a Bréguet 14A2 marked with the black thistle in a red and white pennant of SPA38. Since this unit's duties included reconnaissance missions over the Aisne and Champagne sectors, it included a Bréguet or two among its normal complement of SPAD VIIs and XIIIs

As previously mentioned, one of Madon's disciples was American ace David Endicott Putnam, who was born in Jamaica Plains, Massachusetts, on 10 December 1898. In April 1917 he joined the LFC, and was briefly assigned to N94 in December, before helping to form new *escadrille*, N156.

While serving with the latter unit, Putnam was credited with four confirmed and seven probable victories, some of which he scored

while flying the Morane Saulnier AI parasol fighter, before transferring to SPA38 on 2 June and downing two Albatros D Vs on the same day. Perfecting his skills under Madon, Putnam claimed five Albatros D Vs on 5 June, but only one was confirmed. He was commissioned a first lieutenant in the USAS on 10 June, but was still in SPA38 when he destroyed a two-seater and a balloon on the 15th.

Adjutant André Martenot de Cordoux, who had served with Madon in N38 in 1917, had mixed feelings when SPA94 began receiving SPAD XIIIs in the spring of 1918. For months he kept his nimbler SPAD VII for lone sorties between squadron patrols in the XIII. One of Martenot's squadronmates, Pierre Marinovitch, had fewer reservations about the new fighter, however, and soon eclipsed Martenot as SPA94's top-scorer.

Born in Paris on 1 August 1898, Marinovitch was, according to Martenot, 'of part Serbian extraction, with a Polish mother'. On 12 February 1916, he enlisted in *27e Régiment de Dragons*, but on 14 July he transferred into aviation. Soon after arriving at N38 on 19 March 1917, Marinovitch fell ill, and after spending two months in hospital, he was reassigned to N94.

Martenot remembered that Marinovitch had been 'educated in Paris and in Ireland, and spoke fluent English, which was to stand him in good stead with our later American *escadrille* members. Marinovitch preferred attacking enemy aircraft, and getting citations, to other missions, and he was very good at it, as his 22 victories testified. "Marino" was a good shot,

but not a good pilot. He wrecked a lot of planes. He used no tactics – just charged in and relied on his good shooting. Once he landed too low at the edge of the field, where there was a road bordered by a ridge. He bounced on the ridge and cracked up – that was a typical Marinovitch landing'.

Maréchal-des-Logis Marinovitch scored his first four victories flying Nieuport 24s prior to 30 January 1918, when N94 was ordered to Villeneuve les Vertus and was incorporated into GC18 under Capitaine Jacques Sabattier de Vignolle, along with SPA48, N153 and N155. Promoted to adjutant in February, Marinovitch attacked a two-seater 3000 metres above Caurel on 26 March, and last saw it spinning down trailing smoke when he disengaged at 400 metres. At first credited as a probable, it was confirmed after the war.

On 15 May, Marinovitch brought a reconnaissance aeroplane down near Esserteaux, its crew being taken prisoner. Four days later, he and Sous-Lt Henri Fleureaux of SPA95 sent a Rumpler crashing south of Moreuil. By then, the French press were referring to the 19-year-old Marinovitch as the 'Benjamin des As' because of his youth.

On the 31st 'Marino' downed a two-seater over Villers-Cotterets, its pilot, Unteroffizier Hippolyt Kaminski, being killed and the observer, Lt.d.R Bake of *Flieger Abteilung* (A) 264, being taken prisoner. He also destroyed a Fokker Dr I a few minutes later. On 1 June, Martenot claimed another triplane, whose pilot, Lt.d.R. Rudolf Rienau of *Jasta* 19, came down unhurt near Parcy, and rejoined his *Staffel* the next day. Martenot became an ace on 5 June, when he and Marinovitch shot down a two-seater. On the 9th, Marinovitch forced an enemy two-seater down on its own field at St Paul-au-Bois.

By the end of June, the German offensive had again stalled at a heavy cost to the Allies. For SPA94, that price included its commander, Lt Guy de la Rochfordiére, killed on 11 June by Leutnant Franz Büchner of *Jasta* 13. On 1 July Marinovitch sent a Rumpler down near Monnes. Two days later, Sous-Lt Benjamin Bozon-Verduraz arrived from SPA3 to take command of SPA94.

On 15 July the Germans launched their last offensive at the Marne, and Marinovitch shared in the destruction of two enemy aeroplanes, followed by a Rumpler on the 22nd. Martenot was made a *Chévalier de la Légion d'Honneur* on 5 August, as was Marinovitch on the 11th. Not one to rest on his laurels, 'Marino' added a Rumpler and a Fokker D VII to his tally on the17th. On the same day, Bozon-Verduraz sent a two-seater crashing north-east of Roye, but was then driven down over the frontline by four Fokkers, and probably credited to Vizefeldwebel Gustav Klaudet of *Jasta* 15. On 21 August, Martenot and Adjutant Jean Joseph Ondet came to the aid of a formation of Bréguet 14B2s and shot a Fokker D VII down west of Soissons, killing Vizefeldwebel Anton Bernhörster of *Jasta* 61.

On 8 September, GC18 moved east from Nanteuil-le-Hardouin to a new aerodrome at Autrey, south-west of Nancy. There, the groupe was put at the disposal of Brig Gen William Mitchell in preparation for the first American offensive of the war at St Mihiel.

13 September saw Martenot and Lts Albert Carbonnel and Jean Laganne credited with bringing down a Fokker D VII behind the American frontline near Vieville-en-Haye. This may have been Lt.d.R. Paul Wolff of *Jasta* 13, who was reported to have been (*continued on page 49*)

Sous-Lt Charles Marie Joseph Léon Nuville joined N57 on 25 November 1916, but did not score his first victory until 24 September 1917. Exactly one year later, he scored his 12th, and on 6 November 1918 he was appointed to command SPA154. Retiring from the *Armée de l'Air* in 1945, Léon Nuville died in his native Puybrun on 18 January 1965, aged 75

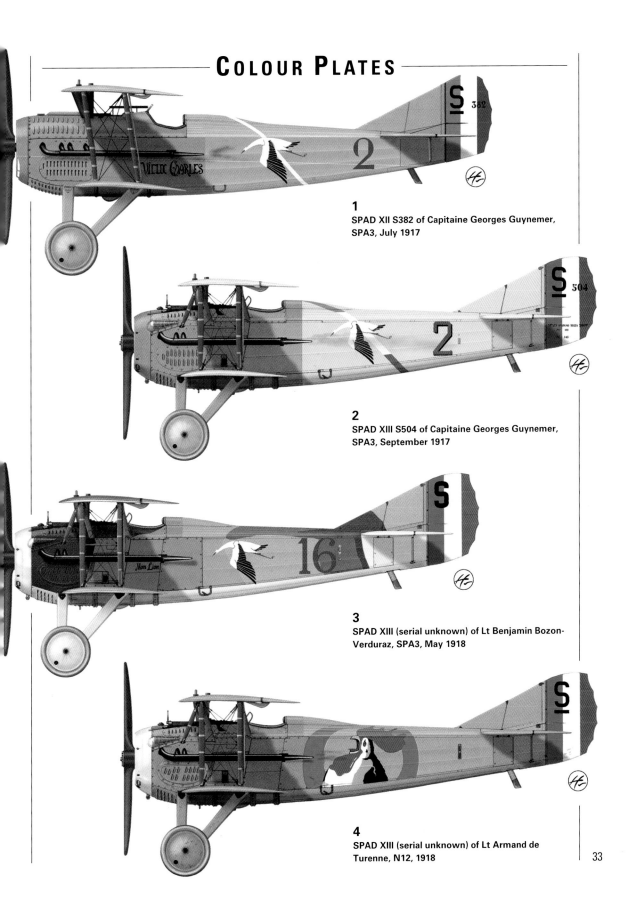

1
SPAD XII S382 of Capitaine Georges Guynemer,
SPA3, July 1917

2
SPAD XIII S504 of Capitaine Georges Guynemer,
SPA3, September 1917

3
SPAD XIII (serial unknown) of Lt Benjamin Bozon-
Verduraz, SPA3, May 1918

4
SPAD XIII (serial unknown) of Lt Armand de
Turenne, N12, 1918

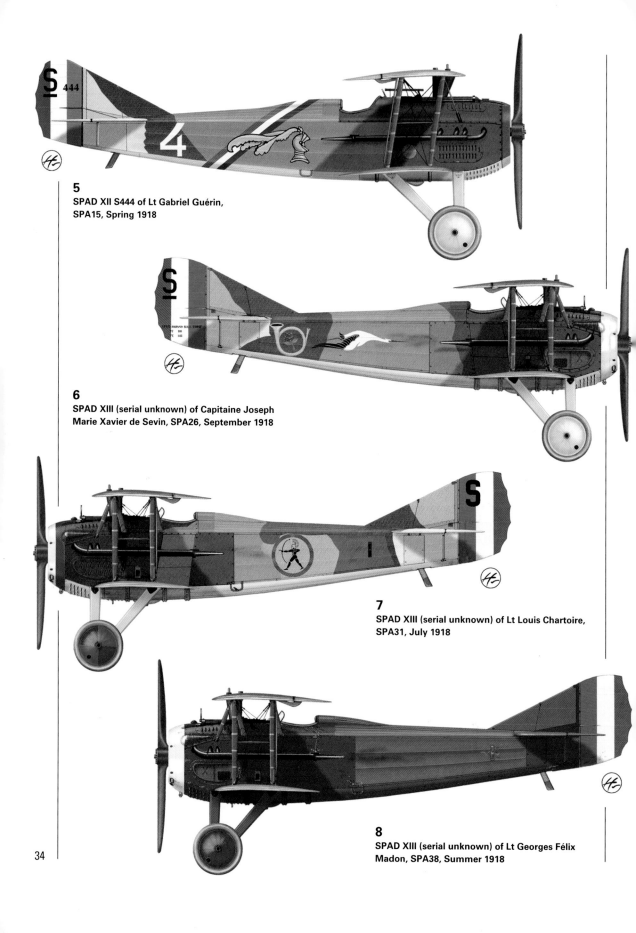

5
SPAD XII S444 of Lt Gabriel Guérin,
SPA15, Spring 1918

6
SPAD XIII (serial unknown) of Capitaine Joseph
Marie Xavier de Sevin, SPA26, September 1918

7
SPAD XIII (serial unknown) of Lt Louis Chartoire,
SPA31, July 1918

8
SPAD XIII (serial unknown) of Lt Georges Félix
Madon, SPA38, Summer 1918

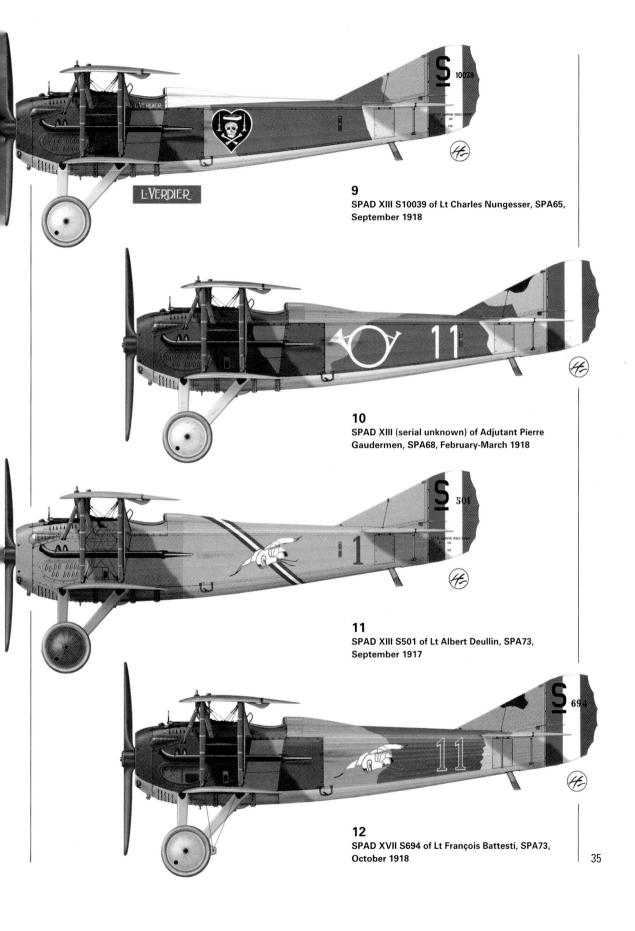

9
SPAD XIII S10039 of Lt Charles Nungesser, SPA65,
September 1918

10
SPAD XIII (serial unknown) of Adjutant Pierre
Gaudermen, SPA68, February-March 1918

11
SPAD XIII S501 of Lt Albert Deullin, SPA73,
September 1917

12
SPAD XVII S694 of Lt François Battesti, SPA73,
October 1918

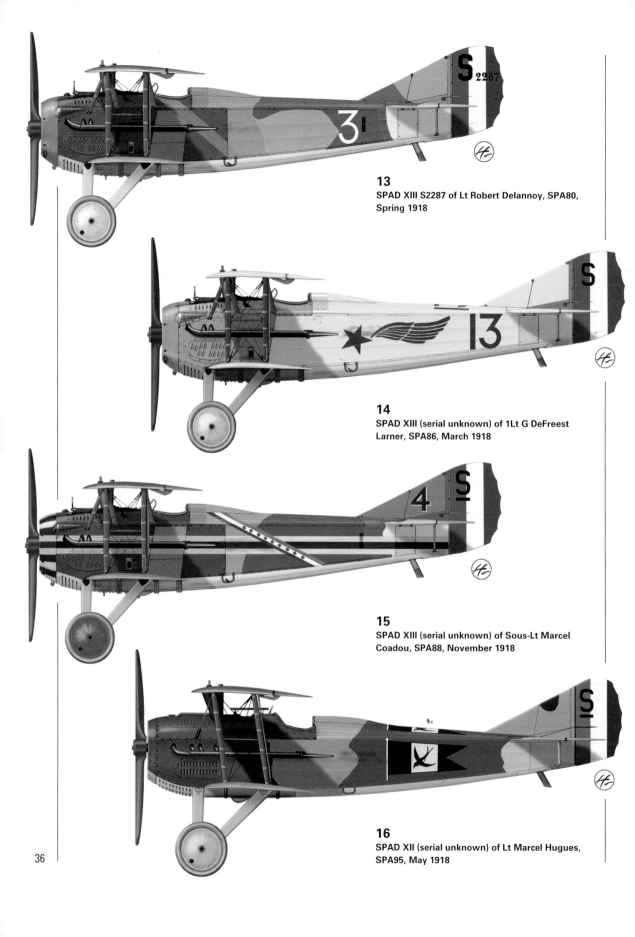

13
SPAD XIII S2287 of Lt Robert Delannoy, SPA80,
Spring 1918

14
SPAD XIII (serial unknown) of 1Lt G DeFreest
Larner, SPA86, March 1918

15
SPAD XIII (serial unknown) of Sous-Lt Marcel
Coadou, SPA88, November 1918

16
SPAD XII (serial unknown) of Lt Marcel Hugues,
SPA95, May 1918

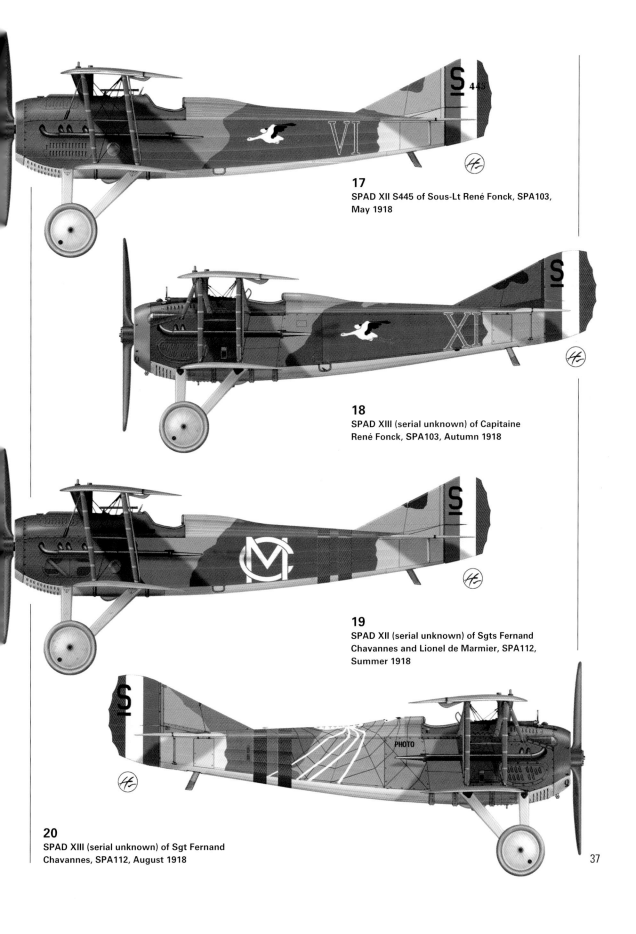

17
SPAD XII S445 of Sous-Lt René Fonck, SPA103,
May 1918

18
SPAD XIII (serial unknown) of Capitaine
René Fonck, SPA103, Autumn 1918

19
SPAD XII (serial unknown) of Sgts Fernand
Chavannes and Lionel de Marmier, SPA112,
Summer 1918

20
SPAD XIII (serial unknown) of Sgt Fernand
Chavannes, SPA112, August 1918

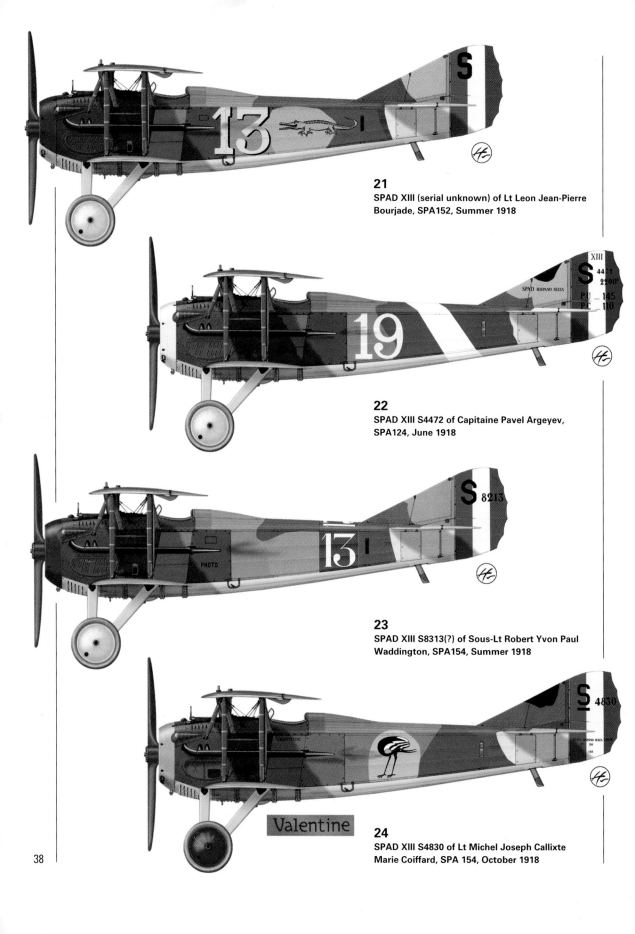

21
SPAD XIII (serial unknown) of Lt Leon Jean-Pierre Bourjade, SPA152, Summer 1918

22
SPAD XIII S4472 of Capitaine Pavel Argeyev, SPA124, June 1918

23
SPAD XIII S8313(?) of Sous-Lt Robert Yvon Paul Waddington, SPA154, Summer 1918

24
SPAD XIII S4830 of Lt Michel Joseph Callixte Marie Coiffard, SPA 154, October 1918

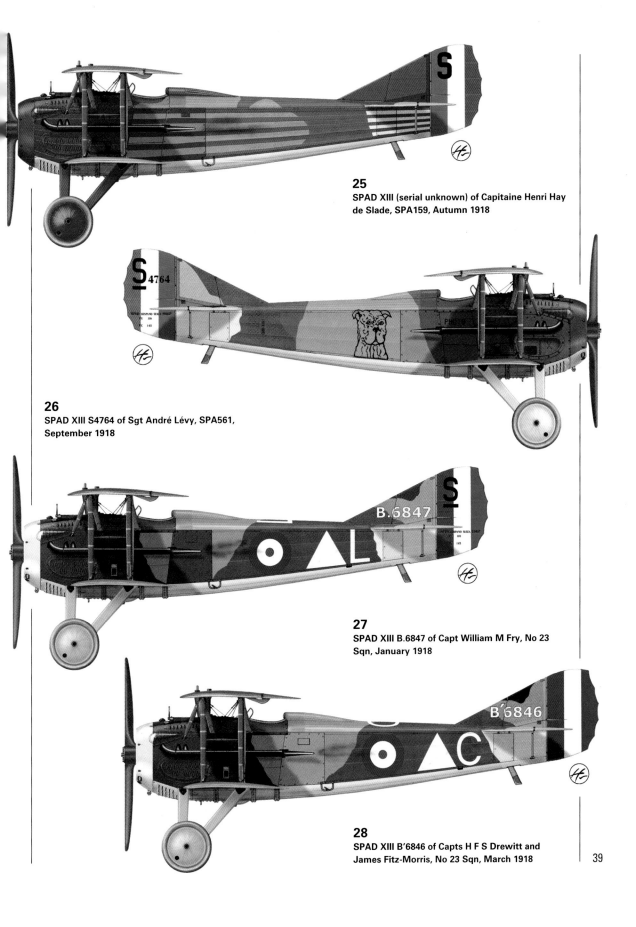

25
SPAD XIII (serial unknown) of Capitaine Henri Hay
de Slade, SPA159, Autumn 1918

26
SPAD XIII S4764 of Sgt André Lévy, SPA561,
September 1918

27
SPAD XIII B.6847 of Capt William M Fry, No 23
Sqn, January 1918

28
SPAD XIII B'6846 of Capts H F S Drewitt and
James Fitz-Morris, No 23 Sqn, March 1918

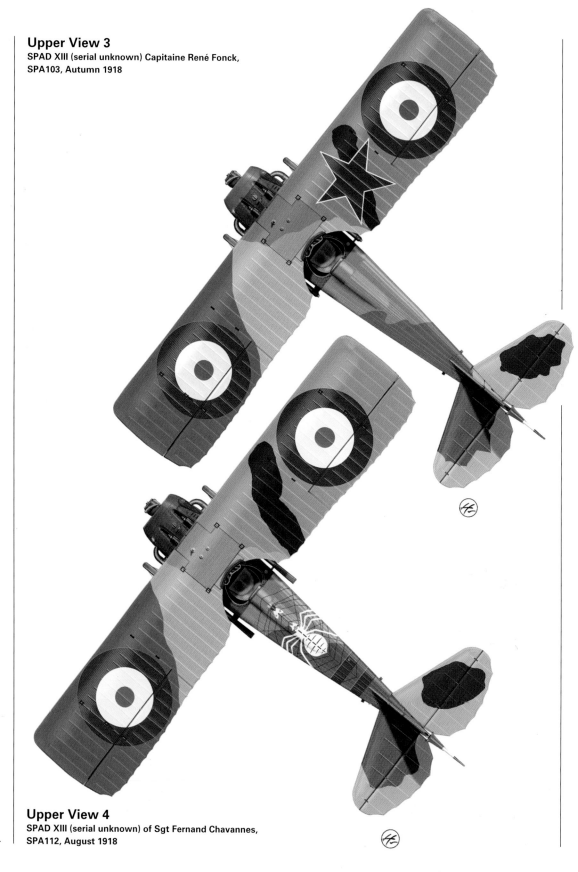

Upper View 3
SPAD XIII (serial unknown) Capitaine René Fonck,
SPA103, Autumn 1918

Upper View 4
SPAD XIII (serial unknown) of Sgt Fernand Chavannes,
SPA112, August 1918

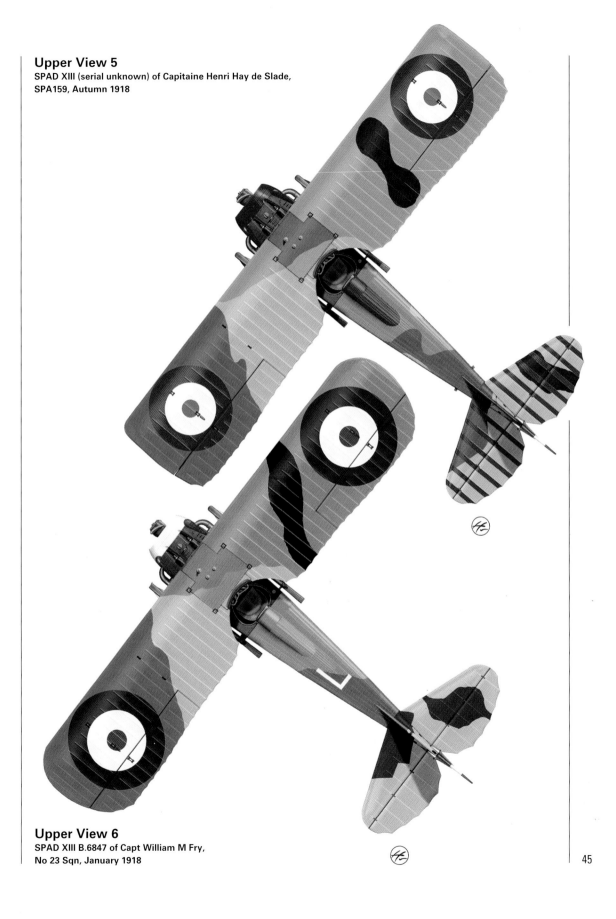

Upper View 5
SPAD XIII (serial unknown) of Capitaine Henri Hay de Slade,
SPA159, Autumn 1918

Upper View 6
SPAD XIII B.6847 of Capt William M Fry,
No 23 Sqn, January 1918

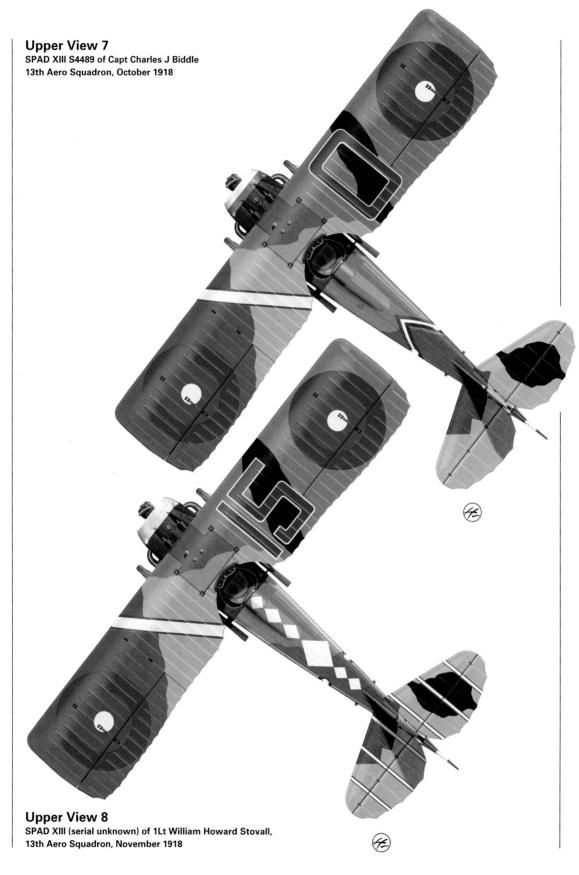

Upper View 7
SPAD XIII S4489 of Capt Charles J Biddle
13th Aero Squadron, October 1918

Upper View 8
SPAD XIII (serial unknown) of 1Lt William Howard Stovall,
13th Aero Squadron, November 1918

Upper View 9
SPAD XIII S15202 of 2Lt Frank Luke Jr,
27th Aero Squadron, September 1918

Upper View 10
SPAD XIII S4523 of Capt Edward V Rickenbacker,
94th Aero Squadron, September 1918

Wing Top Views

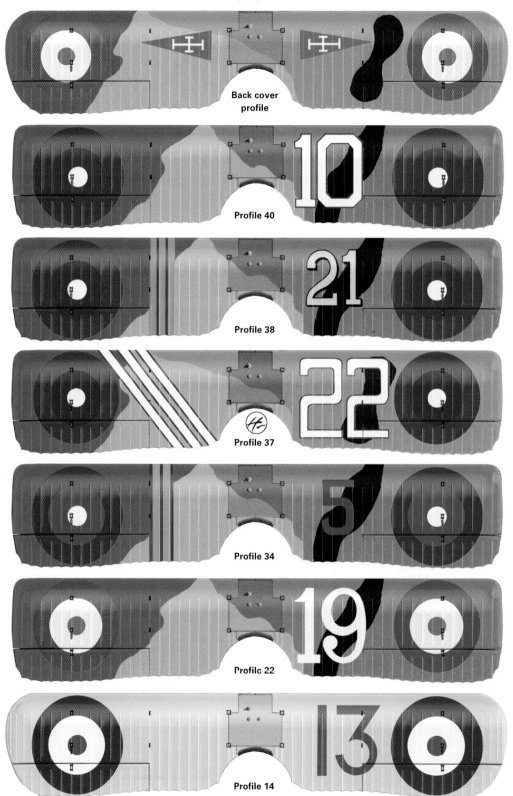

Back cover
profile

Profile 40

Profile 38

Profile 37

Profile 34

Profilc 22

Profile 14

taken prisoner wounded, and his Fokker D VII, with a green nose and a white lightning bolt on a blue fuselage, recovered intact. The St Mihiel offensive concluded on the 18th, and five days later SPA94 moved to Cernon, south of Châlons, to support the *IVéme Armée's* drive to the Meuse.

Bozon-Verduraz inaugurated SPA94's most successful month by downing an enemy aeroplane on 3 October, while Martenot jumped two Fokker D VIIs over St Martin l'Heureux and saw one go down 'at least badly damaged'. Martenot's claim was only counted as a 'probable', but German records reveal that Leutnant Fritz Höhn, the newly promoted commander of *Jasta* 41 with 21 victories, was mortally wounded over St Martin l'Heureux that day. On the 5th, Marinovitch attacked a Rumpler and two Fokker D VIIs, and sent one of the latter crashing east of Challerange, possibly wounding Leutnant Arno Benzler, *Staffelführer* of *Jasta* 60 and a nine-victory ace.

Marinovitch disposed of a Rumpler near Semide on 9 October, while Bozon-Verduraz and Laganne downed a two-seater near Bantheville. On the 18th, Marinovitch and Ondet sent a two-seater crashing behind German lines. On the 27th Marinovitch was commissioned a sous-lieutenant, and he celebrated his promotion by despatching a Fokker D VII in flames near Le Thourn, probably killing yet another German ace, Unteroffizier Karl Schlegel of *Jasta* 45, with 22 victories. On 31 October SPA94 moved to La Noblette, having scored ten victories in one month.

On 3 November, Marinovitch and Adjutant Henri Grimouille sent a two-seater down near Le Chesne for SPA94's 42rd, and last, confirmed

Sous-Lt Robert Joseph Delannoy peers from the cockpit of an early SPAD XIII. The light blue diagonal band under the cockpit was the marking of his *escadrille*, SPA80 (*Steve St Martin Collection via the Author*)

Mechanics work on Delannoy's Blériot-built SPAD XIII S2287 after the ace suffered engine failure and then ran into a power line while trying to force-land. That Delannoy was not seriously injured in the resulting crash speaks volumes for the SPAD's renowned durability (*Steve St Martin Collection via the Author*)

Lt René Paul Fonck poses in the cockpit of his SPAD XIII. France's – and the Allies' – 'ace of aces', Fonck claimed a total of 126 victories, 75 of which were confirmed

Capitaine Henri Joseph Marie Hay de Slade stands beside the SPAD XIII that he decorated with red stripes while commanding SPA159. Leading literally by example, Slade brought the squadron out of a pitiable state and added eight victories to the 11 earlier successes he had amassed while serving in SPA86 (*Éstablissement Cinématographe et Photographique des Armées SPA B0 89*)

success. Credited with 21 victories – later raised to 22 – 'Marino' emerged as SPA94's star performer, while Martenot's score stood at between six and eight. Unfortunately, Pierre Marinovitch was killed in a flying accident at Evére airfield, near Brussels, on 2 October 1919.

Leadership did not always come easy to the aces. René Fonck eschewed it, as did Henri Joseph Marie Hay de Slade, until circumstances left him no choice. Born in Brest on 29 May 1893, Slade had been a cadet at Saint Cyr before the war, serving in the cavalry until he began flight training on 11 May 1916. On 13 December he was assigned to N80, which on 15 March 1917 was incorporated with N75, N83 and N86 into GC14, under the command of Chef de Bataillon Robert Léon Henri Massenet-Royer de Marancour. On 16 April 1917, Slade transferred to SPA86, and he scored his first 11 victories with that unit.

The only other ace to serve in SPA86 was Gorman DeFreest Larner, an LFC volunteer from Washington, DC, who loved the SPADs and scored all of his victories in the XIII. Of Slade, Larner recalled, 'He was quite short, thin and extremely attractive looking. I only flew with Slade a few times. I don't think he was too personal with anyone. A graduate of St-Cyr and apparently well-born, he was aloof at times, particularly from the sous-officiers. Since I was a caporal, and lived with the sous-officiers, I didn't see much of the officers. The only officer I really came close to was Massenet de Marancour. He spoke English, had been to the States and liked Americans'.

Larner's first victory, on 18 March 1918, was a Pfalz D III that fell in flames over Aguilcourt, killing Unteroffizier Kurt Straube of *Jasta* 66. The German spring offensive began three days later, and in the ensuing week GC14's pilots were heavily committed flying ground attack sorties. On 25 March, however, Slade and Larner shot down a two-seater in flames near Noyon, killing Unteroffizier Hans Vick and Lt.d.R. Friedrich

Officers of GC14 are seen between patrols in the spring of 1918. They are, from left to right, Sous-Lt Louis-Joseph Milliat, SPA80 (three victories), Sous-Lt Bamberger, SPA75, Lt Henri Hay de Slade, SPA86 (19 victories), 1Lt G DeFreest Larner, SPA86 (seven victories), Lt Antoine d'Aboville, SPA86 (one victory), Lt Robert Delannoy, SPA80, Capitaine Étienne Thiriez, commander, SPA86 (two victories) and an unidentified pilot

Lohmann of *Fl.Abt.*(A) 206. Not one to lead his groupe from behind a desk, Massenet de Marancour downed an enemy aeroplane over Lassigny for his seventh victory on 12 April.

'When I became a US first lieutenant but remained with SPA86 from February to June 1918', Larner continued, 'I had to move out of the sous-officers' barracks to that of the officers. I was discouraged from resuming my former camaraderie with the sous-officers by my new barracks-mates. I wasn't sorry to leave when Bill Thaw asked me if I would like to transfer over to his 103rd Aero Squadron as a flight commander'.

On 28 July 1918, Slade arrived at Plessis-Belleville, with orders to take charge of SPA159. Since its formation on 16 January 1918, SPA159 had lost 13 pilots killed or taken prisoner – including its commander, Lt Georges Mazimann, who was killed on 20 July by Oberleutnant Bruno Loerzer of *Jagdgeschwader* III – with not one aerial victory in compensation. Joining Slade as his executive officer was Sous-Lt Louis Risacher, who had previously scored two victories in SPA3. 'Slade was a nice companion', Risacher recalled. 'The rest were young pilots who knew nothing about the job. I had to teach them everything. Everything'.

Slade, too, was chagrined to leave his friends at SPA86 for the responsibilities of leading a unit whose morale had hit rock bottom. 'I'd been something of a loner before, and did not know how to impart my techniques to others', he confessed. 'But something had to be done, so I had my SPAD XIII painted all over with prominent red stripes down the fuselage, and before taking the men up on patrol, I told them that in the event of combat they had to stay up and watch what I did – the stripes should have made it easy enough to recognise me in the most confused dogfight.

'Sure enough, we came upon an enemy formation, and I dove into them, deliberately going through all my standard manoeuvres in the course of the fight, during which I shot down one of my adversaries. After a few such "lessons", I let the others join me in combat to apply what they had seen, and it must have worked because from then on 159 started taking a toll of the enemy, while her losses markedly decreased.'

On 11 August, Sgt Priollaud, an experienced transferee from SPA65, scored SPA159's first confirmed victory. Slade resumed his scoring three days later, followed by more successes on 22 August and 2 September. Meanwhile, on 31 August, Risacher engaged German fighters over the

Sgt Chavannes sits in his uniquely decorated Adolphe Bernard-built SPAD XIII of SPA112 in the autumn of 1918. This unit used two red bands around the rear of the fuselage as a squadron marking, while the pilots had their choice of personal identification – and evidently were granted considerable latitude

This Fokker D VII was brought down by Sgt Chavannes at Roziéres-sur-Crise on 18 July 1918. The pilot was probably Leutnant Konrad Schwarz, who was both commander of *Jasta* 66 and a five-victory ace. The Germans admitted his loss on this date, Schwarz being taken prisoner and eventually dying of his wounds on 24 August

Adjutant-Chef Laurent Baptiste Ruamps poses alongside his SPAD XIII, which bears the white cat emblem of SPA87. Born in St Germain du Bel Air on 14 February 1897, Ruamps scored six victories flying Nieuports between 21 August 1917 and 27 March 1918, then raised his tally to ten with the SPAD XIII. Made a *Commandeur de la Légion d'Honneur* in July 1961, Ruamps passed away on 27 July 1972 (*SHAA B88.2683 via Jon Guttman*)

Only 12 days older than Laurent Baptiste Ruamps, Adjutant Lucien Marcel Gasser also scored ten victories with SPA87, half of which were achieved in Nieuport 27s between 16 February and 27 March 1918. Flying a SPAD XIII by the time this photograph was taken, Adjutant Gasser poses for the camera beside a crewman of the Rumpler that he, Sous-Lt Henot and Maréchal-des-Logis Vuillemin brought down at Villers Allerande on 7 July 1918. On 15 July, Gasser was seriously wounded in the left leg, which subsequently had to be amputated. In addition to the *Médaille Militaire* and *Croix de Guerre* with seven *palmes* and one *Étoile de vermeil*, Gasser was made a *Commandeur de la Légion d'Honneur* before his death in a flying accident at Malzéville on 14 February 1939 (*Musée de l'Air via the Author*)

Forêt de St Gobain and shot down two of them.

Promoted to capitaine (temporary) on 13 September, Slade downed an enemy aeroplane north of Suippes on 24 September and two more on 1 October. On 10 October he burned two balloons (one of which was shared with SPA159's LFC member, Sgt Edwin Bradley Fairchild) to bring his total to 19. On 6 July 1919, Slade was made an *Officier de la Légion d'Honneur*, as well as receiving the *Croix de Guerre* with 14 *palmes*, the Belgian *Croix de Guerre*, the Italian *Croix de la Couronne*, and the British Military Cross. Retiring from the *Armée de l'Air* as a colonel, and a *Grand Officer de la Légion d'Honneur*, he died on 2 November 1979.

Several SPAD XIII aces contributed to SPA81's total of 88 victories, including its commander, Lt Adrien Louis Jacques Leps, who probably scored half of his 12 kills in the twin-gun SPAD. Sous-Lt Marcel Marc Dhôme downed at least one German balloon in a SPAD XIII for his ninth victory, and Adjutant Maurice Albert Rouselle used one when he burned a *Drachen* for his fifth victory on 5 October 1918. Squadronmate Sgt Paul Santelli flamed no fewer than seven balloons in 1918.

Sous-Lt Pierre de Cazenove de Pradines of SPA81 had scored five victories in SPAD VIIs when, on 9 December 1917, he was badly wounded below the left knee. Cazenove was relieved to learn that his leg did not have to be amputated, but said that, 'After rejoining my *escadrille* five months later, I was greatly troubled by the vibrations of my aeroplane. I had my mechanic rig an elastic support for my left leg, which I used when taking off, and which relieved me a lot'.

In spite of his handicap, Cazenove added a two-seater to his score, in concert with his longtime partner, Sous-Lt Henri Albert Peronneau, on 1 July. 'On 31 July', Cazenove recalled, 'I took part in a sad action.

Peronneau and I caught another two-seater over Reims, which defended itself well until the observer ran out of ammunition and stood up in his rear cockpit with his arms folded. The pilot dove, but we shot him down. The observer jumped with his parachute, but the pilot was killed in his aeroplane. The observer descended into French territory, but we found out later that he had been captured by Algerians, who castrated him. It was pitiful'.

Cazenove's seventh and Peronneau's ninth victory was probably from *Fl.Abt.*(A) 286b, which recorded the loss of Vizefeldwebel Karl Kastner and Leutnant Hans Schilling over Taissy, east of Reims, that day.

In addition to the 'old hands' who added to their scores in the SPAD XIII, numerous 'lesser lights' used it to gain most, or all, of their successes. Among them were Adjutant Georges Halberger of SPA153, Adjutant Paul Hamot of SPA49, Adjutant Georges Fréderic Lienhart of SPA37, Sgt Paul Montange of SPA155, Adjutant André Marie Paul Petit-Delchet of SPA57, MdL Gilbert Uteau of SPA315 and Lt Pierre Armand Wertheimer of SPA84, all of whom scored five victories in 1918.

THE ABORTIVE SPAD XVII

In early 1918, the *Aviation Militaire* requested a fighter with a more powerful engine than that fitted to the SPAD XIII. Hispano-Suiza responded with the 300-hp 8Fb, while Britain offered the 320-hp ABC Dragonfly radial. Both engines had problems, but SPAD set to work on modifying and strengthening the SPAD XIII airframe to accept the 8Fb. The result was the SPAD XVII.C1, whose dimensions were virtually identical to those of the XIII.C1, but which featured a larger engine cowling and more stringers to round out the fuselage behind it. The wing cellule was reinforced to a factor of nine, with additional bracing wires running under the lower wing to the undercarriage, and the horizontal

SPAD XVII S745 displays the extra stringers and enlarged horizontal control surfaces that helped distinguish the new type from the SPAD XIII
(*SHAA B82.4341 via James J Davilla*)

Only 20 SPAD XVIIs were completed, and most were assigned to *escadrilles* of GC12 – SPA3, in which the aircraft shown here served in the closing weeks of the war, and SPAs 26, 67, 103 and 167
(*SHAA B82.781 via James J Davilla*)

Sgt François Marie Noll Battesti stands before a Blériot XI whilst learning to fly in 1914. After pre-war service in BI18 and BI3, Battesti flew Caudron G IVs with C10 until he was seriously wounded on 6 July 1916. After retraining in fighters, he returned to the front with N73 on 12 March 1917. Of Battesti's seven credited victories, at least three were scored in SPAD XIIIs and one in a SPAD XII. The Corsican-born ace also flew a SPAD XVII in the last weeks of the war

stabilisers were enlarged. The first SPAD XVII was completed in April 1918, but due to teething troubles with the 8Fb engine, it had a 220-hp Hispano-Suiza 8Be installed when Capitaine Slade test-flew it.

The SPAD XVII's performance proved to be only marginally better than the SPAD XIII's, and a test batch of just 20 was produced before the *Aviation Militaire* decided to adopt the Nieuport 29 as its standard fighter for 1919. Most of the SPAD XVIIs went to GC12, including S682, which was allotted to SPA103 and evaluated by its leading ace, René Fonck. Lt François Battesti, SPA73's seven-victory ace, is also known to have applied his personal number '11' to S694.

FLYING FOREIGN LEGIONNAIRES

As with the SPAD VII, many notable exponents of the SPAD XIII in the *Aviation Militaire* were not French, but volunteers who had enlisted via the Foreign Legion or the *Lafayette* Flying Corps. Most of the Americans eventually transferred to their own army or naval air arms in 1918, but some preferred to remain with the French.

The famous all-American *Lafayette Escadrille*, SPA124, produced several aces, but only one, Gervais Raoul Lufbery, scored all (16) of his victories with that unit prior to his death on 19 May 1918. After SPA124 became a French unit, it produced one other ace, but curiously he too was a foreign volunteer – from Russia.

Born in Yalta, in the Crimea, on 1 March 1887, Pavel Vladimirovich Argeyev was a lieutenant colonel in the Imperial Russian army who happened to be in France when war broke out. Resigning his Russian commission, he enlisted in the Foreign Legion as an infantry lieutenant on 12 September 1914. Wounded twice, Argeyev – or Paul d'Argueev, as the French spelled it – was promoted to capitaine and, on 7 May 1915, he was made a *Chevalier de la Légion d'Honneur* for valour under fire. Shortly afterward, he was again wounded and declared unfit for infantry duty.

Argeyev's response was to request a transfer to aviation, earning his military pilot's certification at Avord on 30 January 1916. He was assigned to N48 on 1 June, but in mid-July he was sent to the Eastern

Capitaine Pavel V Argeyev stands before his SPAD XIII S4472 '19' in late June 1918. At least six of the nine victories he scored with SPA124 were achieved in SPAD XIIIs. Those, added to the six he had been credited with in the Imperial Russian Air Service in 1917, made the Crimean-born volunteer the *escadrille's* only ace of 1918 *(SHAA B87.3829 via the Author)*

Front and assigned to the 1st Fighter Group of the Imperial Russian Air Service, led by Rotmistr Aleksandr A Kozakov. On 27 February 1917, Argeyev shot down an Albatros two-seater, and scored two more victories in April. He and his group commander teamed up to shoot down Albatros two-seaters on 9, 10 and 21 June, raising Argeyev's tally to six and Kozakov's to 13. Following the Revolution, and the signing of the Treaty of Brest-Litovsk by the Bolsheviks, Argeyev left for France in April 1918, and was assigned to SPA124 on 11 May.

'Capitaine Argeyev was obviously older than the band of little sous-lieutnants of which I was part', recalled squadronmate Marcel Robert, 'and besides, he was our superior officer. He was nonetheless quite close to us – he liked to joke around and let himself be kidded and joked with, particularly over his errors in French, which he spoke approximatively.

'Capitaine Argueev wasn't a refined pilot,' Robert continued. 'Very rough in his piloting, but an extraordinary warrior and hunter. He only liked to fly and fight alone. Considering his background, our squadron commander left him entirely free to fly when and as he pleased.

'Being of Slavic temperament, he had fits of passivity, sometimes waiting days to just watch us fly or sleep in the sun. Then, when the fit passed, he would leave alone to hunt. Argeyev had the "eye of the hunter" to an extraordinary degree, discovering game when we couldn't find it. As soon as an adversary revealed himself, he would charge at full speed, diving to break everything, without making the slightest manoeuvre, and would not fire until he had closed to point-blank range. And thus, he had more victories than any of us over *"l'idiote Boche"*, as Argeyev called the enemy.'

He destroyed an enemy aeroplane south-east of Reims on 1 June, and scored again on the 13th, 14th and 26th. After a 'dry spell', he downed a Fokker D VII over Cerney on 27 September, followed by two two-seaters on the 28th and another on 5 October. His 15th kill, a two-seater east of Quatre Champs on 30 October, was also the 26th and last for SPA124 – with no pilots lost since its return to combat as a French squadron.

After the war, Argeyev joined the *Compagnie Franco-Romaine*, flying the commercial route between the Czechoslovakian capital Prague and the Polish capital Warsaw, but on 30 October 1922 he became disoriented in bad weather and crashed into a mountain near Trutnow, on the German-Czechoslovakian border. He was killed in the accident.

Another Russian ace, Viktor Georgiyevich Federov, was born in Verny, Turkestan, on 11 November 1885, but his affiliation with the Social Democratic Party, regarded as revolutionary by the Czarist government, forced him to move abroad, and he was residing in France when the war began. Wounded while serving in the Foreign Legion before going into aviation, Sgt Federov flew Caudron G IVs with C42. During his time with the unit, he and his observer, Cpl Pierre Lanero, were credited with three enemy aeroplanes destroyed in March 1916 before Federov was wounded again on 3 April. Commissioned a sous-lieutenant on 9 August, the 'Flying Cossack of Verdun', as he was called, served in N26 before departing for the Romanian front in October.

In March 1918, with Russia out of the war and political factions for which he could muster little sympathy vying for power, Federov returned to France and was posted to SPA89 in June. Made a *Chevalier de la Légion d'Honneur*, he joined Adjutant Emile Julien Mathurin Regnier and three

Russian-born Lt Viktor Georgiyevich Federov scored his first three victories while flying Caudron G IVs with C42 in March 1916, then served on the Eastern Front, mainly as an instructor. Although a socialist, he became disillusioned with the Russian Revolution and returned to France on 16 May 1918, where he scored two more victories with SPA89. He died of tuberculosis in St Cloud on 4 March 1922

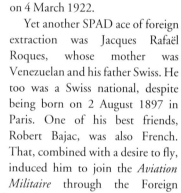

other pilots in shooting down a reconnaissance aeroplane near Bar-le-Duc on 18 September. Regnier, who had previously scored three victories in SPAD VIIs, shared in two more on 25 and 26 September. While escorting Allied bombers on 9 October, Federov downed an enemy fighter over Damvillers for his fifth and SPA89's ninth and final victory, but he was wounded while fighting three Fokkers the next day, and possibly credited to Vizefeldwebel Albert Haussmann of *Jasta* 13. Retiring to Paris, Viktor Federov died of tuberculosis at Saint-Cloud on 4 March 1922.

Yet another SPAD ace of foreign extraction was Jacques Rafaël Roques, whose mother was Venezuelan and his father Swiss. He too was a Swiss national, despite being born on 2 August 1897 in Paris. One of his best friends, Robert Bajac, was also French. That, combined with a desire to fly, induced him to join the *Aviation Militaire* through the Foreign Legion when war broke out. Posted to N48 on 2 January 1917, Roques scored his first two victories in the SPAD VII. Early in 1918, he received a SPAD XIII, which he considered 'solid and very manoeuvrable, but with a tendency to lose speed very quickly on landing. But it was easier to land than a Farman if you came in slightly tail-down'.

On 19 February 1918 Sgt Roques, his friend Sous-Lt Bajac – who was also serving in SPA48 – and Sgt Edmond Caillaux sent a Rumpler down in flames over Nogent l'Abesse, killing both Vizefeldwebel Adolf Schulz and Leutnant Erich Richter of *Fl.Abt.*(A) 203. Promoted to adjutant, Roques scored next on 12 June, when he and Adjutant Émile Quiles downed a Fokker D VII in flames near Ressons-sur-Matz, killing Leutnant Rudolf Croissant of *Jasta* 68.

Five days later, Roques teamed up with Lt René Montrion and Adjutant Caillaux against a Halberstadt CL II over Chaudun, hitting the observer with his first volley and then sending the aeroplane down. Their claim, corresponding to the deaths of Unteroffiziere Paul Nickel and Friedrich Witschakowski at nearby Ambrief, was Roques' fifth, Caillaux's fourth (to which he would later add a fifth) and Montrion's 11th victory. During a balloon attack at Villiers Helon on 28 June, however, Montrion was ambushed by a Fokker D VII and died at age 21, probably the victim of Leutnant Karl Bolle, commander of *Jasta* Boelcke.

Although he scored no more aerial victories, Roques was awarded the *Médaille Militaire* for identifying and strafing a German machine gun nest on Hill 101 in support of the *28e Régiment des Dragons*, and similarly assisting a patrol of the *6e Cuirassiéres* in capturing an enemy emplacement between La Boissiére and Grivilliers. Roques became a French citizen in 1919, was made an *Officier de la Légion d'Honneur* in 1936, and during World War 2 served as a capitaine in GC I/1, whose Bloch 152s bore the old cockerel's head insignia of his old unit, SPA48. After France's surrender in June 1940, Roques worked with the Resistance, and in post-war years became an artist and photographer. He died in May 1988.

Fellow 'foreigner' Bernard Artigau was also French by birth, having been born in Licq-Arthery in France's Basque country, but his family emigrated when he was young, and by 1914 he was an Argentine citizen. Even so, after war broke out Artigau, declaring to his Argentine friends that he was still 'French at heart', boarded a ship for Bordeaux in 1916, and enlisted in the *144e Régiment d'Infanterie*. He soon developed an interest in aviation, however, and in June 1917 he joined SPA15.

Sgt Artigau scored his first official victory near Livry-sur-Meuse on 4 September, and on 1 November, he and Lt Charles Calamai sent a Rumpler crashing into the trenches near Reservoir, killing Flieger Ernst Graf and Leutnant Max Bartel of *Flieger Abteilung* (A) 206. On 23 December Artigau and Sous-Lt Gabriel Guérin claimed a DFW C V and its crew, Leutnants Willy Müller and Max Winterfeld of *Fl. Abt.*(A) 248, the aircraft falling in pieces behind German lines.

On 2 February 1918, Artigau and Guérin sent a two-seater down in flames over Beine, killing Unterof-fizier Otto Gumz and Leutnant Karl Otto of *Fl.Abt.*(A) 203. Artigau became an ace on 11 April, when he caused a Rumpler to crash in German territory near Montdidier, killing Flieger Gottfried Aberle and Leutnant Wilhelm Schuleit of *Fl.Abt.*(A) 271. The very next day he forced a two-seater down at

This view of S727 reveals that the corners of its early, rounded wings were squared off using plywood pocket extensions. In spite of this modification, which the Royal Flying Corps rejected, Roques liked S727, scoring his fourth and fifth victories in it on 12 and 17 June 1918 (**SHAA B81.2129 via the Author**).

Born in the Basque country of France in 1894, but an Argentine citizen when he returned to volunteer for French service in 1916, Adjutant Bernard Artigau scored 12 victories with SPA15. His Blériot-built SPAD XIII displays an asymmetrical white triangle on the fuselage upper decking, and the name *Jeannette* below the cockpit. Unfortunately for modellers, Artigau's personal fuselage number is not shown in the photograph (**SHAA B76.1832 via the Author**)

The first day of August began with a triple balloon victory for Coiffard and Ehrlich north of Somme-Py, while a fourth fell to Waddington, Chevallier and Barbreau at 1750 hrs. Coiffard and Barbreau burned balloons on the 3rd, and on 9 August a Fokker D VII fell victim to Waddington, Chevallier and 1Lt Alvin H Treadwell, a USAS pilot temporarily attached to the *escadrille*. Ehrlich scored a solo balloon victory on 10 August, and the next day he and Coiffard destroyed another. In addition, Coiffard and Petit downed a Fokker D VII while en route to the balloon target, and Coiffard downed another Fokker on the return flight.

While flying in close formation shortly afterward, Ehrlich was blinded by sun glare on his goggles and ran his propeller into Waddington's SPAD. Ehrlich managed to glide down, but Waddington spun down several hundred feet before regaining sufficient control to land safely. At that point, Coiffard, recognising signs of combat fatigue in Ehrlich, ordered him away for a month's leave. Waddington, on the other hand, continued his best-scoring month by downing a fighter over Caudry on 21 August.

On 22 August, Sous-Lt Théophile Henri Condemine joined SPA154, and while flying his first mission that same day, he destroyed a balloon in concert with Waddington and Gros. Born in Champagnac-Fontaine on 25 January 1895, Condemine had served in the hussars and infantry before being badly wounded on 29 July 1917, and then transferred into aviation. Condemine destroyed another *Drachen* in a solo attack on 7 September 1918, and on the 14th he, Coiffard and Cpl Marcel Lisle burned two more at Gernicourt and Cormicy.

Meanwhile, Ehrlich had returned, and on 15 September he joined Coiffard and Condemine in a lightning attack that eliminated three *Drachen* in less than six minutes and caused the observer of a fourth to take to his parachute. In spite of their successes, the pilots of SPA154 were also reminded of their mortality on 15 September. Coiffard's SPAD was hit and he had to force-land near Trepail. Then, at 1640 hrs, MdL Raymond Mercklen was killed by anti-aircraft fire. Five minutes earlier, Sous-Lt Louis Gros, at that point credited with nine victories, had been wounded in the thigh by a Fokker D VII over Bethancourt, and after struggling back over the lines, he force-landed at Lhéry and was evacuated to hospital. The balloon buster's 'Law of Averages' had begun to catch up with SPA154, and it would take a greater toll three days later.

At 1806 hrs on 18 September, Ehrlich, Petit and Sgt Charles Peillard burned a balloon at Brimont after three low-level passes, but as they headed for home, they were jumped by 11 Fokkers D VIIs of *Jasta* 66. Peillard managed to escape, but Petit, victor over two German aircraft and five balloons, was shot down, soon followed by Ehrlich – either by the Fokkers or by ground fire while trying to evade them. Petit died of his wounds shortly after being captured, while Ehrlich spent the rest of the war as a 'guest of the Kaiser'.

Coiffard burned a balloon south-east of Semide on 28 September and destroyed a two-seater south-east of Atienne on 2 October. Condemine's last two victories, on 3 and 10 October, were also the last balloons credited to SPA154.

Coiffard led a patrol to escort a reconnaissance aeroplane on 28 October, but while en route to the rendezvous the French encountered a *Staffel* of Fokker D VIIs. Coiffard attacked, but only Condemine saw his hand

Assigned to SPA154 on 22 August 1918, Sous-Lt Théophile Henri Condemine shared in the destruction of a balloon with Sous-Lts Waddington and Louis Gros on the same day. He added six more 'gasbags' to his score in September, and had raised his tally to nine by 10 October. Condemine went on to serve in World War 2, reaching the rank of lieutenant colonel

Born in Pau on 5 April 1898, Adjutant Charles Jean Vincent Macé served in the dragoons and artillery before transferring to aviation on 22 July 1917. Posted to N90, he opened his account with two enemy aeroplanes, in concert with Adjutant Ruamps of N87, on 27 March 1918. He did not score again until 14 August, but his tally rose steadily thereafter to 12, including eight balloons. Awarded the *Médaille Militaire* and the *Croix de Guerre* with seven *palmes*, Charles Macé was killed in a flying accident at Haguenau, in Alsace, on 7 June 1919

After scoring his first two victories in Nieuports, Sous-Lieutenant Marius Jean-Paul Elzéard Ambrogi probably flew a SPAD when he scored his third victory over a two-seater on 16 May 1918, and he went on to burn 11 balloons between 17 May and 18 October. Flying Bloch 152s with GC I/8 in 1940, he added a Dornier Do 17 to his score during the Battle of France, and had risen to the rank of lieutenant colonel by the end of World War 2

signal and joined him. In the melée that ensued over Château Porcien, Coiffard scored his 33rd and 34th victories, while Condemine claimed a third Fokker that went unconfirmed. Coiffard, however, was struck in the thigh, while a second bullet passed through his back, lungs and out his chest. Covered by Condemine, the iron-willed Coiffard flew 12 kilometres before landing near St Loup-en-Champagne, six kilometres inside French lines. He was given a blood transfusion during the ambulance ride to Berenicourt, but it was not enough – three hours later, Coiffard breathed his last. The following day, he was made an *Officier de la Légion d'Honneur*.

Henri Condemine survived the conflict and went on to serve in World War 2, reaching the rank of lieutenant colonel. Jacques Ehrlich, who had been proposed for the *Légion d'Honneur* after his 'hat trick' of 15 September, but was not awarded it after being taken prisoner, received the *Croix de Guerre* with eight *palmes* and one *Étoile de vermeil*, as well as the *Médaille Militaire*. He, too, served during World War 2, as a member of the French Resistance. Ehrlich died in Paris on 10 August 1953.

The sort of team effort characterised by SPA154 was repeated in the quieter *VIIIe Armée* sector in Alsace-Lorraine by SPA90. There, Sous-Lt Marius Jean-Paul Elzéard Ambrogi often flew SPAD XIIIs alongside Adjutants Maurice Bizot, Charles Jean Vincent Macé and Jean André Pezon to destroy most of the 11 balloons that were added to the previous three aircraft he had shot down. For their roles in those actions, Bizot was credited with ten victories, Macé with twelve and Pezon with ten.

Macé was killed in a flying accident at Haguenau, in Alsace, on 7 June 1919, while Bizot suffered a similar fate on 27 November 1925. Ambrogi went on to fly Bloch MB 152s with GC I/8 during World War 2, downing a Dornier Do 17 in 1940. He later became president of France's veteran fliers' organization, *Les Vieilles Tiges*, prior to his death on 25 April 1971. Pezon, who ultimately became a *Commandeur de la Légion d'Honneur*, died on 24 August 1980, aged 82.

Another noted French balloon specialist, Maurice Jean-Paul Boyau, had enjoyed pre-war fame as captain of the French rugby team. Born in Mustapha, Algeria, on 8 May 1888, he began the war as a truck driver, but commenced flight training late in 1915. After serving as an instructor at Buc, his appeals for a combat assignment finally led to his joining N77 in September 1916. Flying Nieuports, he scored ten victories (including six balloons) between March and September 1917, adding an 11th on 1 October flying a SPAD VII.

Boyau's first balloon of 1918 fell near Beney on 3 January, and his second, on 20 February, was shared with another of SPA77's leading scorers, Sous-Lt Jean Marie Luc Gilbert Sardier. Born in Riom on 5 May 1897, Sardier had scored his first victory on 7 November 1916 and his second (a balloon), on 3 June 1917, had also been shared with Boyau. Sardier shared in the destruction of three Albatros scouts on 15 May, and teamed up with Sergent François Guerrier to burn a balloon the next day.

Boyau flamed another *Drachen* over Bois de Bôle on 29 May, and on the way back he and Sardier downed an Albatros D V. Boyau added a Pfalz D IIIa to his score on 1 June, and three days later he and Sardier destroyed two more *Drachen*. Boyau burned a 'gasbag' on 27 June, teamed up with Sous-Lt Claude Haegelen of SPA100 to eliminate another on 1 July, and on the 5th he again claimed a balloon and a fighter.

Aircraft fell to Boyau's guns on 15, 17 and 21 July, followed by two more balloons, shared with Guerrier, on the 22nd. Boyau downed a trio of aeroplanes on 8 August, and on 14 September he joined Haegelen of SPA100 and LFC member Cpl Edward Corsi of SPA77 to flame a balloon over Etraye. Boyau and three other SPA77 pilots burned two more *Drachen* the next day, raising his total to 14 aeroplanes and 20 balloons.

On 16 September, Lt Boyau, Corsi, Cpl Walk and Aspirant Cessieux went after a *Drachen* at Harville. Boyau and Cessieux destroyed the balloon, but then the French pilots were jumped by seven Fokker D VIIs of *Jasta* 15. Cesseiux and Corsi were wounded, but both escaped. Boyau evaded his first attacker and then,

Assigned to N90 on 10 October 1917, Sgt Maurice Bizot opened his account on 27 March 1918, assisting squadronmate Sgt Charles Macé and Adjutant Laurent Ruamps of N87 in the destruction of two enemy aeroplanes on 27 March 1918. His first SPAD victory was a balloon shared with Ambrogi on 30 July, to which he added two more balloons and an LVG two-seater in August. More team efforts against balloons on 2 September, 21 October and 29 October brought Adjutant Bizot's total up to ten. He was killed in a flying accident on 27 November 1925

Sous-Lt Jean Marie Luc Gilbert Sardier leans against his SPAD XIII of SPA77 in the spring of 1918. His personal number '8' seems to have been applied in gold, highlighted by black or red, while the vertical and horizontal stabilisers have been painted white. Gilbert Sardier scored 12 victories with SPA77 before being given command of SPA48 on 5 July 1918. He scored two more victories whilst leading the unit (*SHAA B76.1869 via the Author*)

Left
SPA77 was known as 'Les Sportifs' because of the many athletes in its ranks, including its leading ace, Sous-Lt Maurice Boyau, who was credited with 15 enemy aeroplanes and 20 *Drachens*. His outstanding career as a fighter pilot came to a fiery end minutes after he had flamed his 20th balloon on 16 September 1918. Boyau's penchant for balloon busting is reflected in the Le Prieur rocket tubes he has had mounted on the interplane struts of his early Blériot-built SPAD XIII, which features a medium blue number '9' as well as the *escadrille's* insignia of a gold Cross of Jerusalem on a blue pennant
(*Imperial War Museum*)

Lt Léon Jean-Pierre Bourjade of SPA152 interrupted his studies for the priesthood to become the leading balloon buster of all time, claiming 27 *Drachen* and one German fighter destroyed
(*SHAA via James J Davilla*)

after diving under the burning balloon, tried to drive a Fokker off Walk's tail, only to be hit by either another German fighter or ground fire. Boyau fell in flames and was credited to Leutnant Georg von Hantelman, but his sacrifice had not been entirely in vain – Walk, though credited to Vizefeldwebel Gutav Klaudet, made it to Allied lines before force-landing his damaged aeroplane.

Gilbert Sardier, who survived the war with 15 victories (five of which were over *Drachen*) became an *Officer de la Légion d'Honneur*, and was also awarded the *Croix de Guerre* with nine *palmes*, one *Étoile de vermeil*, one *Étoile d'argent*, as well as the British Military Cross. He also served as president of the Association Nationale des As before his death on 7 October 1976. Awarded the *Médaille Militaire* and the *Croix de Guerre* with three *palmes* and one *Étoile de vermeil* for five balloon victories (including two on 3 September 1918), François Guerrier died on 28 June 1969.

The highest-scoring balloon-buster of France – or of any country, for that matter – had had aspirations of being a Catholic missionary when war broke out. Born in Montauban on 25 May 1889, Léon Jean-Pierre Bourjade served in the artillery and in a trench mortar unit before transferring to aviation in 1917, and being assigned to N152 on 13 September. Although the unit's crocodile insignia appeared on at least one of Bourjade's SPAD XIIIs, on 27 January 1918, he wrote in his diary of a more personal touch that he had in mind. 'I have asked for a banner from Sacré-Coeur to fly from my machine. The banner has now arrived, and now it is my biggest desire to let it flutter in the air above me'.

The very next day, the Sacré-Coeur pennant was flying from the headrest of Bourjade's Nieuport as he attacked a balloon, only to suffer a gun jam. The same problem frustrated several further attempts, by Bourjade, who after two years in the trenches cowering under artillery fire directed by German balloons had declared that 'the day I could bring one down in flames, it would be more than just a victory. It would be revenge'. Finally, on 27 March, Bourjade dived on a balloon near Gebersweiler, fired and as he pulled up amid a barrage of tracers and shells, he had the satisfaction of seeing it catch fire.

Bourjade now had 'balloon fever', burning three more by 20 May. After completing a three-week gunnery course at Cazaux, he returned to his *escadrille* in June to find that it had transferred from Alsace-Lorraine to the hotter Champagne front, and been re-equipped with SPAD XIIIs. Bourjade came into his stride when he flamed a balloon near St Étienne á Arnes on 25 June, followed by another on the 28th. He shot down a Fokker D VII the next day, and he finished the month by burning a balloon at Rosiéres and attacking a second before jammed guns and engine trouble forced him to disengage. Bourjade teamed up with two squadronmates to destroy yet another balloon on 5 July, and then burned one solo on the 8th.

On the day the Germans launched their final push along the Marne – 15 July – Bourjade eliminated three of their balloons. Two days later he flamed another north of Nauroy, and escaped an enemy fighter patrol despite his SPAD being riddled with bullet holes. His guns jammed and he was wounded in the arm while attacking a balloon near Tahure on 19 July, but he continued diving as it was winched down to 300 metres, at which height he finally cleared his weapons and set it on fire.

After three weeks in hospital and eight days' leave visiting his parents, Bourjade teamed up with Sous-Lt Ernest Joseph Jules Maunoury to destroy balloons on 30 August and 1 September. Three days later, he, Maunoury and Cpl Étienne Manson flamed another, and on 15 September he and Maunoury burned two more. Another double 'sausage roast' with Bourjade over Orainville on 1 October brought Maunoury's total to 11, and Bourjade teamed up with other SPA152 pilots to burn more balloons on 3, 4, 8 and 27 October.

Bourjade's diary entry for 29 October recorded his last victories – and the loss of a friend. 'In the Serancourt region I flamed a balloon at 1100 hrs. I destroyed another at 1125 hrs, protected by (Sous-Lt Henri) Garin and (Sgt Gerard) Fos. Afternoon – I had two combats with Fokkers, with uncertain results. Had to break off, myself. At 1550 hrs, Garin attacked a balloon at low altitude. When returning, I fought off a patrol of four or five Fokkers. At 1620 hrs, we met five other Fokkers. I attacked one, but the guns stopped immediately. After me, another SPAD attacked. I saw it above the enemy and closing in. At that moment, it exploded and fell in the St Fergeux region. It was the SPAD piloted by Garin'.

Henri Garin, a fellow student for the priesthood, who had assisted Bourjade in four of his balloon victories, was credited to Oberleutnant Robert Hildebrandt of *Jasta* 53 as his sixth victory.

Bourjade drove a Fokker D VII down smoking on 31 October, but it was not confirmed. Étienne Manson was shot down in flames by Leutnant Herbert Mahn of *Jasta* 72s during a dogfight over Château Porcien the next day, and on 2 November Bourjade recorded his last combat, an inconclusive attack on four Fokkers.

At the time of the Armistice, Bourjade had flown 254 hours and 45 minutes over the frontline, and had engaged in no fewer than 67 combats, during which he was credited with one enemy fighter and an all-time record 27 balloons destroyed. He was made an *Officier de la Légion d'Honneur*, and also received the *Croix de Guerre* with 17 *palmes* and one *Étoile de vermeil.*

After the war, Bourjade returned to Switzerland to complete his religious studies. His last flight, in September 1920, was a sightseeing joyride for a vicar and a Papuan missionary in violation of an order prohibiting civilians to fly in military aircraft. After finally attaining the priesthood on 26 July 1921, Bourjade served at a leper colony on Yui Island in British New Guinea, but in October 1924 he fell ill and died on the 22nd.

Other French balloon specialists included Claude Haegelen of SPA100, 12 of whose 22 victories were over *Drachen* in 1918, and Maréchal-des-Logis Pierre Desiré Augustin Ducornet of SPA93 who, in addition to a Pfalz on 29 May and a Rumpler on 15 July 1918, destroyed five balloons between 9 August and 29 September.

In contrast to the 20-year-old Ducornet, pre-war aviator Adjutant-Chef Antoine Laplasse was 34 when he joined SPA75 on 20 October 1917, but he downed German two-seaters on 15 December 1917 and 13 March 1918, followed by a balloon on 18 June and two more on 17 August. With four squadronmates flying top-cover, Laplasse burned three *Drachen* near Saint-Gobain on 22 August, and was going after a fourth when five Fokker D VIIs suddenly plunged through his flight, killing Sgt Gentil and then sending Laplasse down in flames.

Even among balloon busters, noted for their individual quirks, it would be difficult to find a more unlikely ace than the devout, bearded Jean-Pierre Bourjade, but the United States managed to produce a unique eccentric of its own. His father may have been German, but only the American West could have produced a character like Frank Luke.

Born on 19 May 1897, and raised in Phoenix, Arizona, Frank Luke Jr was the son of a Prussian immigrant who ruled his wife and children with an iron hand. Young Luke grew up resentful of authority, but he embraced the free environment of the west, becoming an accomplished horseman, a star athlete in school and a dead shot with the rifle and pistol. After the United States declared war on Germany, Luke eagerly enlisted in the Army Signal Corps on 27 September 1917. He found flight school a bore, but worked hard and proved to be a natural pilot. Shipped off to France, 2Lt Luke trained further at the 3rd Aviation Instruction Centre at Issoudun, where he met a man whose name would soon be closely associated with his own – Joe Wehner.

Born in Boston, Massachusetts, on 20 September 1895, Joseph Fritz Wehner was, like Luke, the son of a German immigrant. Although he enlisted in the Army soon after the United States entered the war, he found himself frequently under investigation as an enemy agent. Nothing came of it, save to leave Wehner bitter and distrustful of most company. Luke, with his guileless simplicity, became a rare exception.

On 30 May Luke was made a ferry pilot at the American Aviation Acceptance Park at Orly, but he tended to return from assigned flights whenever he pleased, declaring that he had come to fight, not to ferry. His disgusted commander finally obliged him by assigning him to the 27th Aero Squadron of the 1st Pursuit Group, based at Touquin, on 26 July.

Luke soon reinforced an already bad reputation by showing no respect for the older pilots, while boasting of his own achievements to come. The 27th's Canadian-born commander, Maj Harold E Hartney, perceived Luke's attitude as 'the honest confidence of a zealous but none-too-diplomatic boy', but squadronmates shunned him, and 1Lt Kenneth L Porter of the neighbouring 147th Aero Squadron recalled, 'He spent all his leisure time shooting'. Fortunately for Luke, Joe Wehner had been assigned to the 27th in June, so he had one friend. Hartney, too, came to believe that there was talent in the headstrong Arizonan, and tried to exercise patience with him.

On 16 August Hartney led 12 new SPAD XIIIs on an escort mission for Salmson 2A2 bombers of the 88th Aero Squadron, but the SPADs developed engine trouble and dropped out of formation one by one until only two remained – Hartney's and Luke's. The two men had several encounters with enemy aircraft, during which they became separated. When Hartney returned

Leading American balloon buster 2Lt Frank Luke burned his first German balloon on 12 September 1918, and by the 16th, he and his teammate Joe Wehner were the talk of the USAS. Luke is shown beside a Blériot-built SPAD XIII – one of at least five that he 'used up' within a week of braving gauntlets of flak and ground fire to add to his growing balloon tally

Shown while in training at Issoudun in the spring of 1918, 1Lt Joseph Wehner became Frank Luke's closest friend, as well as his 'top cover', when the duo teamed up to ravage the German balloon line in mid-September 1918

A groundcrewman of the 27th Aero Squadron filled in the blue-white yin-yang wheel hub motif on this photograph of Maj Harold E Hartney alighting from his SPAD XIII at Saints aerodrome in mid-August 1918. The Canadian-born commander of the 27th added a red-white-blue fuselage band and a black and white chequered radiator cowl to the regular unit livery. After scoring six victories in FE 2s with No 20 Sqn RFC, Hartney transferred to the USAS in September 1917 and was flying a Nieuport 28 when he downed an Albatros D Va for his seventh victory on 25 June 1918. On 21 August, Lt Col Hartney was given command of the 1st Pursuit Group

to Touquin, he found his pilots waiting to express their relief that he was back and their disgust at the French 'who wished those crocks on us'. Just then, Luke came back, nursing his own faulty engine. He announced, 'I got a Hun'. He could not provide any further details, however, claiming to have been too busy fighting five other opponents at the time.

Nobody believed Luke, and his standing in the 1st Pursuit Group reached its nadir. Hartney took up the matter with his flight leaders, during which 1Lt Jerry Vasconcells also advocated tolerance, noting that Luke impressed him as being fearless. 'It isn't courage exactly', he said. 'He has no imagination. He can't imagine anything happening to him. He thinks he's invincible. If he ever finds himself he may be almost as good as he thinks he is'. Luke was allowed to fly solo patrols until 21 August, when Hartney was promoted to command the 1st Pursuit Group. Capt Alfred A Grant took over the 27th, and tried to reimpose discipline on Luke – with limited success.

Meanwhile, the 16 August incident drove Luke to type up a set of confirmation forms to carry on all future flights. Then, on the evening of 11 September, he overheard Vasconcells expressing his opinion of balloons. 'I think they're the toughest proposition a pilot has to meet. Any man who gets a balloon has my respect, because he's got to be good or he doesn't get it'.

The St Mihiel offensive began the following morning, and when the 27th sent up its first eight-aeroplane patrol, Luke dropped out to attack a German balloon at Marieville. After three passes, he sent it falling on its winch in flames. He then landed near the frontline and had US Army officers sign his confirmation sheet. As he turned to take off, one of them heard Luke mutter, 'Guess that'll hold 'em'.

The real turning point in Luke's career occurred two days later. At 0930 hrs, Luke and 1Lts Leo H Dawson and Thomas F Lennon burned a *Drachen* at Boinville. During a second sortie at 1430 hrs, Luke left his formation to destroy the balloon at Buzy. Eight Fokker D VIIs then attacked him, and suffering from jammed guns, he was only able to escape when Joe Wehner intervened and shot down a fighter, and forced another to land. Wehner then went after a second balloon, only to see a French SPAD destroy it and come under attack by more Fokkers. Wehner came to the rescue yet again, and downed two of the Germans – none of his victories were confirmed on this day, however.

On 15 September, Luke again dropped out of a patrol to destroy two new balloons at Boinville, and again German fighters descended on him. Wehner came to the rescue yet agian, sending a Fokker crashing and driving an Albatros down in a steep dive. This time Wehner's Fokker was confirmed.

On 16 September, Hartney and Grant invited Brig Gen William Mitchell to observe a scheduled raid on the balloon line by Luke and Wehner. The duo duly destroyed one at Reville at 1905 hrs, and after

1Lt Jerry Cox Vasconcells stands beside his Kellner-built SPAD, '13', of the 27th Aero Squadron. A much-respected flight commander, Vasconcells downed five German aircraft and one balloon before being given command of the 185th Aero Squadron, a nightfighter unit equipped with Sopwith Camels, in November 1918 (*via Greg VanWyngarden*)

flak caused them to become separated, Luke burned a second balloon at Romagne at 1920 hrs, while Wehner destroyed a third over Mangiennes. Both of their SPADs returned in need of complete overhauls, but neither pilot suffered a scratch. Gen Mitchell described the action as 'one of the most remarkable feats in the military career of a youngster that was nothing short of amazing'.

Another witness was the commander of the 94th Aero Squadron, 1Lt Edward V Rickenbacker, who described the differences between the two teammates;

'Luke would come back to the aerodrome and excitedly tell everyone about it, but no word would Wehner say on the subject. In fact Joe never spoke, except in monosyllables, on any subject. After a successful combat, he would put in the briefest possible report and sign his name.'

In only five days, the 'Arizona boaster' and the suspected German spy from Boston had become the most talked-about phenomenon in the USAS. On 18 September they set out again and burned two German balloons near Labeuville, but then were attacked by enemy fighters. Luke drove two Fokkers down and then, unable to find Wehner, flew east until he encountered an LVG that was being attacked by Sous-Lt Pierre Gaudermen and Adjutant Reginald Sinclaire of SPA68.

Pierre Gustave Gaudermen, who was born in Paris on 20 October 1882, was a former international rugby champion who had served in the *101e Régiment d'Infanterie*, *escadrille* MF55 and as a flying instructor, before joining N68 on 20 September 1916. 'Duke' Sinclaire, an LFC volunteer in SPA68, remembered Gaudermen as 'one of the best shots in the *escadrille*', as well as its only ace with five victories. He was made a *Chevalier de la Légion d'Honneur* and died in Paris on 20 December 1948.

Sinclaire thought that the LVG crew on 26 September 'evidently had orders to get the pictures. The pilot was very sharp', he recalled. 'We spent two hours stalking that two-seater, which just kept turning away whenever we presented a threat, then would return to his work when we seemed to give up. After three attempts we finally cut him off. At the same time an American SPAD came up under his tail, also shooting, and landed where the German fell'.

The two Fokker pilots Luke brought down apparently survived, but the LVG crew, Leutnants Ernst Höhne and Ernst Schulz of *Fl. Abt.* 36, were killed. Photographed beside the wreckage of his fifth victory in less than half an hour, Luke's face displayed both elation and concern that he expressed the next morning, when he inquired of Hartney, 'Wehner isn't back yet, is he, Major?' Mortally wounded by Leutnant Georg von Hantelmann of *Jasta* 15, the six-victory ace died in a German field hospital hours after being brought down.

Hartney ordered Luke to Orly Field – and nearby Paris – for eight days' leave, but he came back two days early and talked 2Lt Ivan A Roberts into taking Wehner's place as his wingman. On 26 September, the two set out for the German balloon line, only to be jumped by five Fokker D VIIs. Luke drove one down out of control, but Roberts was brought down by Leutnant Franz Büchner of *Jasta* 13 and taken prisoner. Roberts later escaped, but developed a fever and died near Wasselbonne on 14 October.

Upon returning, Luke went away without leave until 27 September. Upon returning to his unit, the ace was reprimanded by his CO, Grant, and confronted with the deserved irony that soon after he had gone AWOL, the squadron had received a request to eliminate a balloon at Lisson. Unable to find Luke, Grant gave the job to Vasconcells, who destroyed it for his third victory.

On the 28th, Luke took off alone without filing a flight plan, destroyed a balloon in its nest at Bantheville and then spent the night with a nearby French balloon company. When he returned the next morning to hand in his combat report, an irate Capt Grant grounded him, only to learn soon afterward that Luke had taken off and was refuelling at the 27th's auxiliary aerodrome near Verdun! He ordered that Luke be placed under arrest, declaring 'I'm going to recommend him for the Distinguished Flying Cross. Then, by God, I'm going to court-martial him!'

Grant then stormed into 1st Pursuit Group headquarters, where Hartney, in a last attempt at compromise between his unruly star pilot and his exasperated squadron leader, told Grant that Luke was slated to attack German balloons the next morning. On 29 September Luke departed Verdun, flew low over American balloon headquarters at Souilly and dropped a message in a cylinder – 'Watch three Hun balloons on Meuse. – Luke.'

There are several accounts of what happened next, but all – including German records – confirm that Luke destroyed all three balloons as promised. As he burned the last *Drachen*, however, his SPAD was hit by its machine-gun battery, commanded by Leutnant B Mangels, and it came down near Murvaux. French witnesses claimed that Luke strafed the German soldiers before finally landing 50 yards from a stream.

2Lt Luke poses by the remains of the LVG C V that he destroyed on 18 September 1918 – his fifth victory in just ten minutes. His face betrays mixed emotions amid the triumph, however – his best friend Joe Wehner has not returned from this mission

When called upon to surrender, the American defiantly drew his pistol and died in the ensuing shootout. It is more likely, however, that Luke's shot was fired to attract help, which arrived too late to save him from bleeding to death from the wounds he had already suffered.

Luke never got his court martial, but he did receive a posthumous DSC with Oak Leaf Cluster – and soon after, he became the first pilot in the USAS to be awarded the US military's highest combat decoration, the Presidential Medal of Honor.

AMERICAN CLIMAX

The US Army Air Service (USAS) received its first SPAD XIIIs in March 1918, and by the end of the war 893 had been delivered to 15 squadrons, as well as a few individual machines serving with reconnaissance units, such as the 91st Aero Squadron. Prior to then, of course, several Americans of the *Lafayette* Flying Corps had already flown the twin-gun SPAD (some of the US SPADs were armed with 0.30-calibre Marlin machine guns, rather than the usual Vickers), and the experience of those who later transferred to the USAS, such as Charles Biddle and DeFreest Larner, would prove invaluable to the newer pilots.

After a relatively easy combat debut over the quiet Toul sector in April 1918, the USAS's Nieuport 28-equipped 1st Pursuit Group suffered heavy casualties over Château Thierry in July – especially at the hands of the late Manfred von Richthofen's Flying Circus, *Jagdgeschwader* I, now commanded by Oberleutnant Hermann Göring. Following the collapse of the last German offensive on 20 July, the 1st Pursuit began replacing its Nieuports with SPAD XIIIs.

The group's 95th Aero Squadron drew first blood in the new fighter on 25 July, when 21-year-old 1Lt James Knowles Jr from Cincinnati, Ohio, who had been a track star and a member of the varsity baseball team at Harvard University before joining the USAS, downed a Fokker D VII near Bouvardes. Later that same day, he and Harvard classmate, 1Lt Sumner Sewell from Bath, Maine, teamed up with 1Lts C S Gill, W H Heinrichs and G W Puryear to down a Rumpler near Villeneve-sur-Fére.

Sewell had previously scored three kills while flying Nieuport 28s, but the most notable success of 25 July was achieved by 1Lt Walter L Avery, whose only prior experience had been night patrols and ground strafing missions in Nieuport 27s with *escadrille* N471. In his first aerial combat, he managed to bring down a Fokker D VII whose captured pilot turned out to be Leutnant Karl Menckhoff, commander of Royal Saxon *Jasta* 72 and a holder of the *Ordre Pour le Mérite* with 39 victories to his credit.

Back in the Toul sector, the 2nd Pursuit Group, led by Maj Davenport Johnson, was formed from the 13th, 22nd, 103rd and 139th Aero Squadrons on 30 June. The group's first victories were scored by SPAD

Original members of the 13th Aero Squadron pose for the camera on 13 July 1918. They are, from left to right, Capt Charles J Biddle, 1Lt Hobart A H Baker, 1Lt C Maury Jones, Lt Col Davenport Johnson (commander, Second Pursuit Group), 1Lt Alton A Brody, 1Lt George Kull, 1Lt Rob Roy Converse, 1Lt Leighton Brewer, 1Lt Charles Drew, 1Lt J J Seerley, F F Taggart (supply officer), 1Lt E R Richards, 1Lt Henry Riley, 1Lt Hugh Ellis (squadron adjutant), 1Lt Guyon Armstrong, 1Lt W C Worthington (medical officer), 1Lt W H Stovall, 1Lt Stuart E Elliott and 1Lt David Howe

VII pilots of the 139th – a Rumpler by 1Lt David E Putnam on 30 June and a Pfalz D IIIa by 1Lt Arthur Raymond Brooks on 29 July. Flying a SPAD XIII, Putnam brought down a Fokker D VII near Flirey on 15 August, and a Rumpler on the 22nd. On 10 September, 1Lt Wendell A Robertson from Fort Smith, Arkansas, destroyed a Pfalz D IIIa near Mardigny for his first of an eventual seven victories.

The 2nd Pursuit Group's other SPAD VII-equipped squadron, the 103rd, had been formed directly from *Escadrille* SPA124 *'Lafayette'* on 18 February 1918, and had since seen action with GC21 near Reims and detached duty over Flanders. Soon after being ordered to Toul on 29 June, the 103rd added a new ace to its roster. On 11 July 1Lt Edgar Gardner Tobin from San Antonio, Texas, teamed up with 1Lt Eugene B Jones to shoot down a two-seater east of Thiaucourt. On 16 July, Tobin led a two-man patrol against six Pfalz D IIIas over Vieville-en-Haye, claiming two shot down and one out of control – one was confirmed, and Tobin was cited for the Distinguished Service Cross.

He added a two-seater to his score on 1 August, followed by a Fokker D VII on the 10th, probably killing Flieger Herbert Koch of *Jasta* 64w. The next day, Tobin led 1Lts George Willard Furlow and Van Winkle Todd in an attack on two Albatros two-seaters escorted by a Fokker, the trio sending one of the former to crash near Flirey. Todd then engaged the other Albatros but was forced to land near Euvenin, where he was taken prisoner. George Furlow, from Rochester, Minnesota, had just joined the

Pilots of the 103rd Aero Squadron stand flanked on either side by unidentified ground personnel. Starting, second from left, are 1Lt Martin F McQuilken, 1Lt Lawrence E Kauffman, Capt G DeFreest Larner, Capt Frank O'Driscoll Hunter, 1Lt Hugo A Kenyon and 1Lt Livingston G Irving

SPAD XIIIs of the 103rd Aero Squadron display racks for four 25-lb bombs under the fuselages. The different coloured cowlings signified flights – red for the first, white for the second and blue for the third – throughout the Third Pursuit Group (via Greg VanWyngarden)

Trained in Foggia, Italy, rather than in France or Britain, 1Lt William Howard Stovall honed his fighting skills under Biddle's tutelage to score six victories. He is shown beside his SPAD XIII '15', which he flew with the 13th Aero Squadron (*Jack Eder Collection*)

Holding a bouquet of flowers that a local French girl had thrust into his hands, Capt Charles J Biddle, commander of the 13th Aero Squadron, poses in front of the Rumpler C IV that he brought down on 16 August 1918

103rd on 25 July, but he would follow up this eventful combat debut with another four victories before the war was over.

Meanwhile, on 29 July the 103rd Aero Squadron's CO, Maj William Thaw, was given command of the 3rd Pursuit Group, comprising the 28th, 49th, 93rd and 213th Aero Squadrons, at Vaucouleurs. Thaw appealed to Maj Johnson to transfer his old unit to the 3rd Pursuit, and on 6 August Johnson exchanged the 49th for the 103rd. Soon after that, Thaw – emulating the *'Cigognes'* of GC12 and the different coloured bands used by the *escadrilles* of GC21 – adopted variations on the 103rd's Indian head motif for the 3rd Pursuit's 28th, 93rd and 213th squadrons.

August saw a calm before the storm over the Toul sector, broken by occasional clashes with local German units. At the 13th Aero Squadron, Capt Biddle was encouraged by the high level of skill and morale of most of his pilots, but tried to stress the importance of team effort and 'discouraging the great tendency for one man to try to dash off by himself and be a hero at the expense of the whole. Any man who leaves a patrol for such a purpose will be put on the ground for two weeks and confined to camp, and if he repeats the performance I shall send him to the rear'.

On 1 August Biddle and 1Lts Harry B Freeman, John J Seerley and William H Stovall got into a melée with some Albatros scouts, during which Biddle suffered repeated gun jams – he had only one weapon operable by the time he emerged from the fray with two bullet holes in one of his wings. All of the pilots returned, however, and although Biddle was not sure of how many opponents they had shot down, he later wrote;

'Next day in comes a report from an observation post that two of them crashed and both have been officially confirmed. The other members of our patrol who took an active part in the fight will share in the confirmations, it being impossible to be sure who fired the shots which brought these Huns down. I was very glad, as you may imagine, to have had a hand in getting the squadron's first two official Huns.'

On 16 August Biddle became an ace when he caught a Rumpler C IV that had been regularly overflying Toul between 0515 and 0600 hrs. Taking off at 0445 hrs and climbing to 17,000 ft until puffs of anti-aircraft fire signalled the Germans' arrival, Biddle spent five to ten minutes positioning himself along their escape route. The Rumpler was flying at the uncharacteristically low altitude of 14,500 ft (perhaps to save fuel) when Biddle dived on it, mortally wounding the observer, Leutnant Max Gröschel of *Fl. Abt.* 46b, and forcing the wounded pilot, Vizefeldwebel Johann Eichner, to land C IV 8301/17 intact at Barxiéres-au-Dames.

The new 213th Aero Squadron opened its account on 2 September, when 1Lts Charles G Grey, Samuel P Gaillard and Richard Phelan downed a two-seater near Essey. Born on 20 June 1894, Charles Gossage Grey had been a reporter for the *Evening Post* in his native Chicago when he interviewed a visiting representative from the American Field Service, who convinced him to join as an ambulance driver for the French army. 'After I was there for a while', Grey remarked 66 years later, 'I decided I wanted to do more than just drive an ambulance, and I went to see Dr Edmond Gros and enlisted in the *Lafayette* Flying Corps'.

Grey served in N93 from 26 November 1917 through to 21 March 1918, flying SPAD VIIs and XIIIs whenever the winter weather permitted, but seeing little action. After being commissioned in the USAS, he served as a ferry pilot until August 1918, when he became a flight leader in the 213th. 'The first one I shot down never saw me', Grey recalled. 'I was flying along when I saw an aeroplane 1000 ft beneath me, so I turned, dove and shot him down. No risk whatsoever'.

The youngest of the 2nd Pursuit Group's squadrons, the 22nd also commenced its scoring on 2 September when 1Lt A Raymond Brooks, who had transferred over from the 139th on 16 August, downed a Rumpler over Armacourt. Two days later, he was leading 1Lts Frank B Tyndall and Clinton Jones Jr on patrol when they saw the 10th Balloon Company's 'gasbag' go up in flames. Giving chase to its attacker, the trio drove the Fokker D VII down behind German lines, wounding Unteroffizier Albert Bader, a Swiss volunteer with *Jasta* 64w. These first kills entitled the 22nd to display an insignia on its SPADs, and Brooks designed its emblem – a shooting star, inspired by memories of a comet he had seen over his hometown of Brookline, Massachusetts, when he was 12.

Brooks regarded the 26-year-old Clinton Jones, who came from San Francisco, as one of the 22nd's best pilots, but the unit's top-scorer began as its least promising member. Born in 1894, Jacques Michael Swaab was the son of Mayer Swaab, a Philadelphia businessman. He joined the USAS shortly after war broke out, but after completing his training at Issoudun, he begged test pilot Temple Joyce to arrange for him to serve alongside him, insisting that he needed more flying time before he felt ready for combat. On his first day as a test pilot, however, Swaab made a perfect landing ten feet above the ground, then pancaked, smashing his aeroplane. On the third day, he ground-looped, breaking both wings. After that, Joyce's commander told him 'For God's sake, send that idiot up to the front. He's safer there than he is back here!'

When Swaab flew his first patrol on 8 September, he balked when his flight went into an almost vertical dive – up to that point, he had flown Nieuports with instructions not to exceed 120 mph in a dive, and nobody had told him that the SPAD XIII was much sturdier. Descending at a more prudent speed, Swaab found himself alone, so he flew west for 20 minutes until he spotted an airfield. As he attempted to land to ask for directions, another aeroplane took off and almost collided with him – and then Swaab noticed the crosses on what he now realised was a Fokker D VII. A strong north-east wind had been blowing all day, and Swaab had made almost no progress on his return flight, thereby ending up over a German aerodrome.

An overall view of Rumpler C IV 8301/17 brought down by Capt Biddle. Its pilot, Vizefeldwebel Johann Eichner, was taken prisoner, but observer Leutnant Max Gröschel of *Fl. Abt.* 46b, died of his wounds

Within 24 hours of being credited with downing two Fokker D VIIs – and being shot down over Allied lines – on 14 September 1918, 1Lt Arthur Raymond Brooks received this new SPAD XIII, S7689, shown here prior to the application of the 22nd Aero Squadron's 'shooting star' insignia. Brooks was probably flying S7689, which he christened *SMITH IV* in reference to the college his fiancée was attending, when he downed a DFW C V over Aincreville on 9 October, for his sixth victory. 1Lt Clinton Jones Jr was flying it on 30 October when he claimed a Fokker D VII over St Georges for his eighth kill. Shipped to the US postwar, the SPAD is on display in the National Air and Space Museum in Washington, DC. Brooks, who helped in its restoration, was the last surviving USAS ace when he died on 17 July 1991

After a shaky start as a test pilot, 1Lt Jacques Michael Swaab had little confidence in his abilities as a fighter, but he nonetheless survived his first combat, on 8 September 1918, with three German kills to his credit. He went on to down seven more enemy aeroplanes to become the 'shooting star' of the 22nd Aero Squadron

Recovering from his shock, he fired at the equally startled German and saw him go down in flames. Swaab's guns then jammed, and as he turned away, he found himself surrounded by a further ten Fokkers. Clearing his jam, Swaab fired at the leading aeroplane and saw it go down in a spin. He then tried to reach the clouds, whilst constantly being fired upon by the other Fokkers until, as he described it, 'an unfortunate Boche got in the way of some American-made bullets and burst into flames'. 'I made the cloud', he added, 'passed away into semi-consciousness and next found myself pinned under my aeroplane'.

Swaab had made it to Allied lines, and a formation of Bréguet 14B2s of the 96th Aero Squadron, returning from an aborted bombing mission, had witnessed his fight and confirmed his three victories. After hearing his account, Temple Joyce asked 'Jack, I can understand how you could just inadvertently figure the right deflection to get a guy, but why the devil didn't they get you?' 'Well, Temp', Swaab replied, 'you know I can't fly, and when the sons of guns aimed at me, I was either skidding or slipping, and never got to where they were firing!'

Mid-August saw the 1st Pursuit Group join the two newer groups back in the Toul sector to participate in the first major American operation of the war. Gen John J Pershing, commanding 665,000 troops in 19 divisions, backed by 3220 guns and 267 tanks, aimed to drive the ten divisions of Gen Max von Gallwitz's *Armee Gruppe C* from the region around St Mihiel. Pershing had also amassed 1476 aircraft, including attached French groupes and even three Italian Caproni bomber units, under the overall command of Brig Gen Billy Mitchell. Although not officially attached to Pershing's First Army, the nine Royal Air Force bomber units of Maj Gen Hugh Trenchard's Independent Force also lent voluntary support.

On the ground, the offensive exceeded expectations. The Germans knew they were in a dangerous salient, and were withdrawing when the Americans struck on 12 September, capturing some 15,000 men and 257 guns, and liberating 200 square miles of French territory in six days. This encouraging, but deceptively easy, success cost Pershing only 7000 casualties – one-third of what the Army Medical Corps had anticipated.

In the air, the Allies achieved supremacy by sheer weight of numbers at a proportionately higher cost. The local German *Jagdstaffeln* had been bolstered by the arrival of the veteran JG II under Hauptmann Oskar von Bönigk, comprising *Jastas* 12, 13, 15 and 19, and consequently the Americans saw plenty of action in which a number of aces were made and several lost. A post-war examination of German records has revealed that while the USAS emulated the French practice of awarding shared kills to each airman as a whole victory, rather than in fractions, it was much less strict than the French in confirming their claims. That policy produced a multitude of successes on paper, but the statistics were deceiving in regard to how effective the USAS really was in eliminating its opposition.

Rain and thunderstorms marred the first day of the offensive, but the SPAD units flew whenever they could. One such squadron was the 93rd. At 1020 hrs on 12 September, 23-year-old 1Lt Leslie J Rummell from Newark, New Jersey, claimed a Fokker D VII over Thiaucourt, but then became lost in cloud, ran out of fuel and had to crash-land. Nearby, 22-year-old 1Lt Charles Rudolph D'Olive from Suggsville, Alabama,

with 300-hp Hispano-Suiza engines will probably be in use.'

In spite of that pessimistic report, many of the American SPAD XIII pilots were coming fully into their stride in October. Rickenbacker burned a balloon on the 1st and at 1730 hrs the next day, he and 1Lt Reed McKinley Chambers brought Hannover CL IIIa 2392/18 of *Schlachtstaffel* 5 down intact near Montfaucon, Visefeldwebels Paul Holtmann and Fritz Hankner being taken prisoner.

One of the classic photographs of World War 1 shows leading USAS ace Rickenbacker posing with his Kellner-built SPAD XIII S4523 at Rembercourt on 18 October 1918. Note the 'star-spangled' wheel cover

Rickenbacker and Chambers were each credited with Fokker D VIIs ten minutes later, and at 1815 hrs 1Lt Hamilton Coolidge, who had scored his first victory while flying a Nieuport 28 on 7 July, shared in bringing down a Halberstadt two-seater. Rickenbacker claimed a Fokker D VII on 3 October, while Coolidge became an ace by destroying another D VII and a balloon, then teaming up with Rickenbacker and the 95th Aero Squadron's 1Lt Edwin Peck Curtis to down an LVG.

The following day Charles Grey of the 213th claimed a Fokker for his third victory, while DeFreest Larner of the 103rd added an oak leaf to his DSC when he led a four-aeroplane flight into a formation of seven Fokkers and downed one of them over Montfaucon. That same day Monk Hunter came to the aid of seven Bréguets under attack by ten Fokkers and downed two of them, for which he was awarded a third oak leaf to his DSC. Two days later he took on six more Fokkers over Bantheville, downing one and scattering the others, and earning a fourth oak leaf.

'It would be an injustice to put me in the same class as Monk Hunter – so much my superior as a fighter boy', Larner remarked in 1978. 'He was a true dare-devil. I was not. I tried to keep my flight members, or others I might be leading, out of trouble (being surprised or at a disadvantage) in combat if possible. I wasn't stodgy – just careful'.

Two aces of the 27th Aero Squadron, Jerry Vasconcells and Donald Hudson, scored their sixth victories on 6 October when they and 1Lt Ernest W Hewitt downed a Fokker D VII over Cuissy. On the 9th, Rickenbacker flamed his third balloon, Jim Knowles of the 95th claimed a Fokker and Ray Brooks of the 22nd teamed up with James Beane and Clinton Jones to score his sixth and final victory.

Larner became an ace on 10 October when he and 1Lts J Waddell and C H Monroe downed a Hannover CL III near St Juvin. That same day, Gen Mitchell despatched the 27th, 94th and 147th Aero Squadrons to eliminate two balloons at Dun-sur-Meuse and Aincreville. Rickenbacker chose Chambers and Coolidge to attack the 'gasbags' at 1550 hrs, while the rest of the group covered them. The Germans were equally determined to defend their *Drachen*, however, and elements of JG I gave the Americans what Rickenbacker called 'a regular dogfight', in which he claimed two Fokkers and Chambers one, while a fourth was shared by Coolidge and 1Lt W W Palmer.

1Lt James Dudley Beane was wounded while serving in French *escadrille* SPA69, but he went on to score six victories with the 22nd Aero Squadron. He was awarded a posthumous Distinguished Flying Cross for 'extraordinary heroism' on 29 October, having downed two Fokker D VIIs on this date. Beane was shot down and killed while flying SPAD XIII S7812 '14' the following day

Assigned to the 94th Aero Squadron on 16 June 1918, 1Lt Hamilton Coolidge (above) teamed up with 1Lt James A Meissner to shoot down a Rumpler on 7 July, and he shared in a second victory on 2 October. Twenty-four hours later Coolidge was promoted to captain, and he became an ace when he downed a Fokker D VII, a balloon and an LVG two-seater on the same day. His final confirmed tally came to five aircraft and three balloons. Coolidge was flying S7743 on 27 October when he was killed by an anti-aircraft shell while rushing to the defence of two reconnaissance aeroplanes that were under attack by six German fighters. In addition to a posthumous DSC for that action, Coolidge was awarded the French *Croix de Guerre avec palme*

Kellner-built SPAD XIII S4526 was assigned to the 94th Aero Squadron's 1st Flight on 28 August 1918 and was flown by 1Lts Reed Chambers (shown) and Edwin R Clark. Although one of the 94th's original members, flying Nieuport 28s, Chambers did not begin scoring until 26 September 1918, when he burned a balloon at Nantillois. He ultimately raised his tally to seven, including double victories on 2 and 22 October

The 147th Aero Squadron was also heavily engaged, with 1Lt Kenneth L Porter claiming one Fokker and sharing a second with 1Lt Oscar B Myers and 2Lt Wilbert W White. Another was credited to Capt James A Meissner and 2Lts George A Waters and Ralph A O'Neill, and a fourth fell to 2Lt William E Brotherton before he was shot down in flames. Rickenbacker saw a Fokker on the tail of another 147th member, at which point White turned and rammed the Fokker head-on. 'For sheer nerve and bravery, I believe this heroic feat has never been surpassed', Rickenbacker remarked. 'The most pitiable feature of Lt White's self-sacrifice was the fact that this was his last flight over the lines before he was to leave for the United States on a visit to see his wife and two small children. Not many pilots enter the service with loved ones so close to them!'

Rickenbacker was belatedly going to Brotherton's aid when he saw another SPAD under attack, and recognised its pilot as his former squadronmate, Jimmy Meissner, 'smiling and good-natured as ever, with two ugly brutes on his tail trying their best to execute him'. Joining the chase, Rickenbacker fired a long burst and wrote, 'The Hun fell off and dropped out of control, the other Fokker immediately pulling away and diving steeply for home, and safety'.

For all the claims made over them, the Germans recorded only one Fokker destroyed – that of Lt.d.R. Wilhelm Kohlbach of *Jasta* 10, who parachuted from his aeroplane after colliding with White's SPAD, and was subsequently credited with it as his fifth victory (Rickenbacker claimed to have seen one of the Fokker pilots he shot down take to his parachute, but evidently confused him with Kohlbach). *Jasta* 10 also credited SPADs to Leutnant Justus Grassmann and Lt.d.R. Alois Heldmann, their victims presumably being Brotherton and Meissner, although the latter made it home.

Ironically, Chambers and Coolidge never did get at the balloons that had been their primary targets. At 1410 hrs, however, a SPAD XIII of the 22nd Aero Squadron flew five miles into German territory, fought its way past several enemy fighters and, descending to an altitude of about ten metres, swooped down upon two *Drachen* at Bayonville and Buzancy and burned both in their 'nests'. The pilot, 22-year-old 1Lt Remington DeB Vernam from New York, had previously served with SPA96, sharing in

1Lt Kenneth Lee Porter of the 147th Aero Squadron stands before Nieuport 28 N6256 '15' in which he shared in the downing of a Pfalz D IIIa with five squadronmates on 2 July 1918. His other four victories were achieved while flying the SPAD XIII, his last, a Hannover CL III, being scored in aircraft '21' on 12 October 1918 after he had taken command of 'C Flight' following the death of 1Lt Wilbert W White two days earlier. Porter died in Queens, New York, on 3 February 1988, aged 91 (*Col C R Glasebrook collection via the Author*)

the destruction of a balloon on 12 August. This daring 10 October raid won him the DSC, and he added a Rumpler to his score eight days later.

On 18 October Charles Biddle, Hank Stovall and Stephen Avery downed a Fokker over Bantheville, bringing Biddle's total to eight and Stovall's to six. On the same day, 1Lts D'Olive and William F Goulding of the 93rd Aero Squadron downed a Fokker D VII over Landres, but D'Olive was driven down in Allied territory by another German (possibly Leutnant Wilhelm Seitz of *Jasta* 8) who flew over him, waved and departed. D'Olive's score then stood at four until 18 June 1963, when the third of the Fokkers he had claimed on 13 September was finally confirmed, making him the last officially acknowledged American ace of World War 1.

Sous-Lt Louis Risacher of SPA159 received welcome assistance from another American on 18 October. 'I had a young pilot with me', Risacher said in a 1981 interview, 'and that absurd fellow saw five or six Fokker D VIIs below us. I'd seen them, of course, but I was not in a position to attack. But as soon as he saw them he attacked, so I had to save him. That's why I dove myself to let him get away, but I had all the Huns behind me and above me, and they shot at me for five to ten minutes. Suddenly, I saw a SPAD coming in, shooting. The Germans saw the source of the attack, and one Fokker passed to my left with the SPAD on his tail. The SPAD shot at him and he fell to pieces. It was Claude Haegelen of SPA100.

Pilots of the 147th Aero Squadron. They are, standing, from left to right, 1Lt Oscar B Meyers, 2Lt Arthur H Jones, 2Lt Edward H Clouser (adjutant), 2Lt Ralph A O'Neill (five victories), 1Lt James A Healy (five victories), 2Lt Charles P Porter, Maj Harold E Hartney, commander 1st Pursuit Group (seven victories), Capt James A Meissner, commander 147th Aero Squadron (eight victories), 1Lt Heywood E Cutting, 1Lt James P Herron, 2Lt Francis M Simonds (five victories), 1Lt George H Brew, 2Lt G Gale Willard, 2Lt Cleveland W McDermott and 1Lt Collier C Olive. Squatting, from left to right, 1Lt Walter P Muther, 2Lt Frank C Ennis, 2Lt Louis C Simon Jr, 1Lt G A S Robertson, 2Lt Stuart T Purcell, 2Lt Thomas J Abernethy, 1Lt Horace A Anderson (supply officer), 1Lt Josiah P Rowe Jr, 2Lt James C McEvoy and 2Lt John W Havey (armament officer)

'At the very same moment another SPAD – I knew it was an American aeroplane by its cockades – approaching at full speed, took another Hun and shot him to pieces. I said, "God save America!", and at that moment I put speed to my old SPAD and took a third D VII in a loop – he looked behind at me and fell to pieces and crashed. The others flew away.'

Risacher's 'Yankee' benefactor seems to have been 1Lt Chester E Wright of the 93rd Aero Squadron, who scored his fourth victory over Bantheville at 1100 hrs that day – and whose victim may have been Lt.d.R. Erich Klink of *Jasta* 68, who was killed at that location. Haegelen's opponent went down west of Landres St Georges for his 21st victory. Risacher's fifth victim, which fell over Buzancy, also the 12th and final victory for SPA159.

Born in Readville, Massachusetts, on 1 September 1897, Chester Ellis Wright had attended Harvard University for three years, leaving in February 1917 to join the USAS. Departing for Europe on 23 November, Wright served as a ferry and test pilot before being assigned to the 93rd on 29 July 1918. Wright and 1Lt Henry D Lindsley downed Fokker D VIIs on 15 and 16 September, and on 10 October Wright fought his way through four German fighters to burn a balloon over Beffu, for which he was awarded the DFC.

Wright was only warming up that morning – during a later patrol on the 18th, he shot down a Fokker over Landres at 1530 hrs, and moments later he and 1Lt Lowell S Harding claimed another. Wright teamed up with 1Lts Harold W Follmer and Ralph L Hartman to destroy a Rumpler two-seater over Fontaine on 22 October, and on the 23rd Wright helped Leslie Rummell send a Fokker down in flames over Andevanne. Moments later, Wright was attacked by three more Fokkers, but shot one of them down near Bantheville and drove the other two back over the lines. That action earned Wright an oak leaf to his DSC, and also made him the 93rd's leading ace with nine victories.

On 19 October, 1Lts Monk Hunter and William Thomas Ponder claimed a Halberstadt two-seater, giving the latter (an LFC pilot from Mangum, Oklahoma) his first success since he transferred from SPA163 to the 103rd Aero Squadron on 7 September.

'Wild Bill' Ponder truly lived up to his nickname on 23 October, when he spotted an Allied aeroplane beset by 13 Fokkers and plunged into their midst, shooting down one over Fontaines and scattering the rest. In addition to gaining his fifth victory, Ponder was awarded the DSC. Meanwhile, Hunter and 1Lt Percy R Pyne downed another Fokker over Dun-sur-Meuse, bringing Hunter's total to nine.

During World War 2, Maj Gen Hunter would lead VIII Fighter Command of the Eighth Air Force, retiring from the USAAF in 1946 and finally passing away in his hometown of Savannah, Georgia, on 25 June 1982.

The 93rd Aero Squadron's 1Lt Chester E Wright poses beside his Kellner-built SPAD XIII S7525 '2' (*Jack Eder Collection*)

Reed Chambers of the 94th shot down two Fokker D VIIs on 22 October, bringing his total to seven, while Rickenbacker claimed one and 'Ted' Curtis of the 95th downed another. The following day, Curtis and 'Denny' Holden attacked three German balloons that had been directing artillery fire onto American troops from Montigny, only to encounter enemy fighters, one of which they shot down for Curtis' sixth and final victory. Holden pressed on toward the balloons, and in spite of having to clear jammed guns several times, he burned one at 1705 hrs, for which he was cited for the DSC.

At 1140 hrs on the morning of the 23rd, Jacques Swaab of the 22nd Aero Squadron was flying a patrol when he saw the 7th Balloon Company's 'gasbag' in flames over Cierges. He pursued the Fokker that had attacked it, and sent the D VII down in flames over German territory – its pilot, Leutnant Max Näther of *Jasta* 62, survived. While returning to his flight, Swaab encountered a Rumpler and shot it down as well.

Another German ace, Vizefeldwebel Gustav Klaudat of *Jasta* 15 – then credited with six victories – was wounded in the left arm during a fight with Rickenbacker on the 23rd, and he was still recovering when the war ended. Four days later, Rickenbacker claimed two more D VIIs, one of which he forced down with a disabled engine. As the latter was gliding down to land, however, it was suddenly attacked by another SPAD, which caused it to crash. Rickenbacker was relieved to see the pilot, Lt.d.R. Max Kliefoth of *Jasta* 19, emerge from the wreck uninjured to be taken prisoner, but was profoundly disappointed at losing his opportunity to bring down the Fokker intact.

He and the 94th also suffered a saddening loss that day when Capt Hamilton Coolidge – who had scored his eighth victory over a balloon on 13 October – dived to the aid of two observation aeroplanes under attack by six fighters, only to be struck and killed by an anti-aircraft shell. Coolidge was posthumously awarded the DSC.

Jacques Swaab and Clinton Jones downed a Fokker on 27 October, and later during the same mission Swaab claimed a DFW. The 27th also saw a Hannover fall to Denny Holden's guns, while 1Lt Harold Huston George, a 25-year-old 139th Aero Squadron pilot from Niagara Falls, New York, earned the DSC by attacking four Fokkers and downing two of them over Bantheville.

At 1530 hrs on 28 October, Capt John Hambleton led six SPADs of the 213th against four Fokkers over Bantheville, only to be jumped by eight more Germans. The Americans managed to fight their way out, during which Hambleton sent a Fokker down in a nose-dive, 1Lt Patrick H Mell caused another to spin away out of control and Charles Grey downed a third in flames for his fourth victory.

The following morning, at 0835 hrs, Leslie Rummell of the 93rd downed a Fokker D VII over Grandpré for his seventh and last victory.

1Lts Lansing C Holden Jr, George Gale Willard and Winthrop N Kellogg stand beside Holden's Nieuport 27 (N5382) while serving in N471 at Le Bourget in April 1918. Holden designed the unique camouflage for this aeroplane, which formed the letters *LCH NY* (L C Holden, New York) on the right tailplane. After joining the 95th Aero Squadron on 20 July, 'Denny' Holden opened his account on 29 September 1918, and on 4 November he scored his seventh, and final, victory. Five of his kills had been over balloons

1Lts Sumner Sewell and Edwin Peck Curtis of the 95th Aero Squadron relax between patrols. Born in Bath, Maine, Sewell scored seven victories, and later served as a state senator and as Governor of Maine from 1941 to 1945. 'Ted' Curtis claimed five of his six victories in SPAD XIIIs, and went on to attain the rank of major general in the US Army Air Forces during World War 2. He died in Rochester, New York, on 13 March 1987, aged 90 (*via Greg VanWyngarden*)

Stenseth of the 28th sent a Fokker crashing north-east of Verdun at 1530 hrs that afternoon, and ten minutes later he joined French ace Adjutant Arthur Marie Marcel Coadou of SPA88 in pursuit of a second Fokker. 'That "Kraut" could fly', Stenseth later remarked. 'He led me all over the sky. I had to use about 200 rounds. Then I couldn't get in a fatal burst, so I had to show him I could fly better than he could. I forced him down in our territory near Consenvoye'.

Vernam and 1Lt Frank B Tyndall downed a DFW C V at 1255 hrs on the 29th, and Swaab and Beane claimed another at 1540 hrs. Forty minutes later, Beane led his flight down on eight low-flying Fokkers over Aincreville, and in the ensuing fight he was credited with downing one in flames and sharing a second with Vernam, bringing both of their scores to six, while Swaab and Jones claimed a third Fokker. Their opponents were probably from *Jasta* 6, which claimed two SPADs, whose pilots, 1Lts John C Crissey and Frank B Tyndall, landed safely in Allied lines, while suffering the loss of Lt.d.R. Martin Fischer, killed near Montfaucon.

The 139th had more mixed fortunes during a wild fight with *Jasta* 74 that afternoon – 1Lts Harold George, Edward M Haight and Karl Schoen were credited with two Fokkers over Damvillers at 1520 hrs, but Schoen, whose score then stood at seven, was killed soon after.

Eddie Rickenbacker burned two balloons on 30 October, making him the undisputed American 'ace of aces' with 26 victories, while 1Lt Harvey Weir Cook, a 94th member from Indiana, attacked three LVGs. In spite of having to clear several gun jams, he brought one down in flames for his seventh victory – and added an oak leaf to the DSC he had earned in the course of scoring his first victory on 1 August. In addition, Bill Ponder of the 103rd Aero Squadron downed a Fokker, Denny Holden of the 95th burned a balloon and Edward Haight of the 139th scored his fifth kill on the 30th, but the 22nd lost two aces during a run-in with *Jasta* 12.

Clinton Jones claimed a Fokker over St Georges for his eighth and final victory before being attacked in turn, shaking off his assailant and returning with 27 bullet holes in his SPAD. Beane, however, was killed by Vizefeldwebel Otto Klaiber (the German's fifth victory), and Vernam was downed by Leutnant Bertling. Wounded in the groin, Vernam was found by the Red Cross in the hospital at Longwy, where the Germans had left him when they evacuated the town, but he died on 1 December.

On 31 October Swaab chased an LVG over the front before his bullets struck home, causing it to explode in mid-air east of Verdun. That brought Swaab's total to ten, making him the 'shooting star' of the 22nd Aero Squadron.

On 3 November Charles Grey became the 213th Aero Squadron's sole ace when he and six squadron-mates burned a balloon at Verriers. Denny Holden also destroyed a balloon on 3 November, and the following day he dived after another as

Leslie Rummell sits in the cockpit of SPAD XIII S7650 '14', which was normally flown by 1Lt Ralph L Hartmann, while Chester Wright leans on the lower wing. Rummell was credited with six victories while Wright, with nine, was the highest scorer of the 93rd Aero Squadron (*Jack Eder Collection*)

Fellow 213th Aero Squadron pilot Roland W Richardson identified SPAD XIII '27' as being flown by 1Lt Charles G Grey, who is shown here with it at Vaucouleurs on 1 September 1918. The Indian head insignia has yet to be applied, but the cowling and cylinder fairings are painted blue with white trim to signify its assignment to the 3rd Flight. Besides being the squadron's only ace, Richardson noted that 'Chas was a good guy – he was my flight commander, and I *know*'. 1Lts Richardson and Samuel P Gaillard shared in Grey's second victory – a Fokker D VII out of control over Sponville on 14 September

Blériot-built SPAD XIII S15250 was usually flown by 1Lt John C Knowles Jr, a native of Cincinnati, Ohio, who scored five victories with the 95th Aero Squadron. He received the Distinguished Service Cross and Oak Leaf Cluster, as well as the French *Croix de Guerre* (*N H Hauprich via the Author*)

it was being winched down through a cone of anti-aircraft fire until he set it alight, also damaging its 'nest' and some adjacent buildings. That action earned Holden his seventh victory, and an oak leaf to his DFC.

Charles Grey received the DSC for an action on 4 November when, leading three SPADs of the 213th, he drove off 12 Fokkers that were attacking bombers of the 96th Aero Squadron. 'Germans attacked a flight of Bréguets', he later commented, 'so we just attacked the Germans and drove them off. It was all very fast – I don't deserve a medal for that'.

'On 4 November 1918', wrote DeFreest Larner of the 103rd, 'my "B Flight" reached its peak. We were on patrol when I spotted a *Staffel* of seven Fokkers, and I led my flight into a favorable position between them and the sun. All this time, the Germans gave no indication that they had seen us – they could not have been a very experienced outfit. When all was ready, down we went, and we stayed above the Fokkers throughout the fight that followed. We shot or drove all seven of them down, of which three were officially credited – one to 1Lt John Frost, one to 1Lt Herbert B Bartholf and I, and one to me alone. The last was also the 32nd, and last, victory for the 103rd since it had officially joined the AEF in July 1918. Not one of us had been touched'.

After the war, DeFreest Larner was a co-founder of the New York Air National Guard, and he served as US Air Attaché in London during World War 2. He died in Easton, Maryland, on 20 May 1984.

Sumner Sewell teamed up with 1Lt Albert J Weatherhead of the 95th to destroy a balloon over Boinville on 4 November, and on the 5th he burned another over Hannonville for his seventh victory. Four days later, he saw a Fokker D VII land at the 95th's advance field at Verdun, and with two squadronmates, he ran up with his pistol drawn to capture the German pilot, Leutnant Heinz von Beaulieu-Marconnay of *Jasta* 65, who claimed to have become disoriented in the fog and mistook the American airfield for his own. Beaulieu's Fokker D VII 4635/18 has been restored and is currently displayed near Ray Brooks' SPAD XIII at the National Air and Space Museum. After his discharge from the Army in February 1919, Sewell served as a state senator during the 1930s, and as Governor of Maine from 1941 to 1945. He died on 26 January 1965, aged 67.

Harold George of the 139th became an ace on 5 November, sharing a Fokker D VII with 1Lts John J Quinn and 2Lt Thomas Ash Jr. During World War 2, Brig Gen George gained greater fame as commander of the Bataan Air Force, improvised from what remained of the US Army Air Corps in the Philippines. Although he escaped to Australia before Bataan fell on

9 April 1942, George was injured in a aeroplane crash at Darwin on 29 April and died the next day.

On 6 November, Jim Knowles of the 95th downed a Fokker over Stenay for his fifth victory. On the same day, Stenseth teamed up with 1Lts Hugh C McClung and Ben E Brown of the 28th to claim a two-seater over the Forét de Woevre, bringing his total to eight, but McClung suffered engine failure and was injured when he crash-landed near Bethelainville. Brown

1Lt George A S Robertson poses in the cockpit of 1Lt Thomas J Abernethy's hybrid SPAD XIII, which combined Kellner wings, a Bernard fuselage and a Blériot tailplane and vertical stabiliser. Also shown is the 147th Aero Squadron's insignia – based on 'Mickey', the rat terrier of former commander Maj Geoffrey Bonnell – and the placement of the red-outlined white numerals on the fuselage and upper right wing. Robertson scored one victory during the war, while 'Abe' Abernethy was credited with three

was then attacked by Fokkers of *Jasta* 6, wounded and captured. 'The four Fokker pilots who chased me down came to Loupy le Château to shake hands with me', he reported. 'Leutnant (Ulrich) Neckel was their flight commander. He told me who he was, and then complimented me for getting the biplane. They seemed to be a very sporty lot of pilots'.

'When the war ended on 11 November 1918, we were all sitting there in very bad weather', recalled Charles Grey. 'Nobody was flying – fortunately – and we could hear the artillery fire at the Front, which was 16 kilometres away. At 1100 hrs, when the war was supposed to end, it stopped – like that. There were only one or two shots after that, which drunken artilleryman must have let off. And that was the end of the war. Everybody was serious business. When the war ended we were all drunk'.

Grey spent most of his post-war years residing in Paris, and gave up flying, 'which', he remarked in 1981, 'may be why I'm still alive'. It is somewhat ironic then that Grey was killed in a hit-and-run automobile accident in Palm Beach, California, in May 1988.

Among the many comments made of the war's last day, it may be fitting to leave the last word to French SPAD ace Pierre de Cazenove de Pradines, whose last patrol over the 'deserted, ravished countryside' of France on 10 November left him with 'a melancholy remembrance'.

'But the memory which I have kept is mostly exultation', he added. 'If I fought with all my heart to liberate my country, I cannot say that I ever had real hatred for my adversary. I consider that he was serving his country (as goes the powerful English proverb, 'Right or wrong – my country!') and I worked to destroy as many as possible.

'The rest was magnificent sport. Our aeroplanes were marvellous implements (well, not always!), and there was a freedom of movement and an independence which is not known nowadays – comrades of the first quality for whom one wept all too often! Finally, an existence to magnificent responsibilities when one was only 20 years old – marvellous memories!'

'Star-spangled' postscript. Capt Reed Chambers shows off the American flag colours applied to his SPAD XIII for the Third Air Carnival at Koblenz in June 1919 (*US Air Force Museum*)

APPENDICES

French Air Force *Escadrilles* known to have been equipped with the SPAD XII

SPA3, SPA12, SPA15, SPA38, SPA48, SPA65, SPA73, SPA103, SPA112, SPA153, SPA159

Note
A single SPAD XII was also assigned to 1Lt David E Putnam of the 139th Aero Squadron USAS and subsequently to Capt Charles J Biddle of the 13th Aero Squadron between Putnam's death on 12 September 1918 and 11 November 1918

French Air Force SPAD XIII *Groupes de Combats* in 1917-18

GC11 – SPA12, SPA31, SPA57, SPA154, SPA165
GC12 – SPA3, SPA26, SPA67, SPA103, SPA167, SPA173
GC13 – SPA15, SPA65, SPA84, SPA88
GC14 – SPA75, SPA80, SPA83, SPA86, SPA166
GC15 – SPA37, SPA81, SPA93, SPA97
GC16 – SPA78, SPA112, SPA150, SPA151, SPA168
GC17 – SPA77, SPA89, SPA91, SPA100 (plus Hd174 equipped with Hanriot HD 3C2s)
GC18 – SPA48, SPA94, SPA153, SPA155
GC19 – SPA73, SPA85, SPA95, SPA96
GC20 – SPA68, SPA99, SPA159, SPA162
GC21 – SPA98, SPA124, SPA157, SPA163, SPA164, SPA175, (plus 103rd Aero Squadron USAS, March-May 1918)
GC22 – SPA38, SPA87, SPA92, SPA152, SPA16
GC23 – SPA82, SPA158, SPA160, SPA161, SPA170

Additional SPAD XIII-equipped *Escadrilles*

SPA23, SPA49, SPA62, SPA69, SPA76, SPA79, SPA87, SPA90, SPA102, SPA156, SPA171, SPA313, SPA314, SPA315, SPA412, SPA442, SPA461, SPA462, SPA463, SPA464, SPA466, SPA467, SPA469, SPA470, SPA471, SPA472, SPA506, SPA507, SPA523, SPA531, SPA561

RFC SPAD XIII Squadrons in France in 1917-18

No 19 Sqn, June – July 1917 (a few SPAD XIIIs may have been used alongside the unit's normal complement of SPAD VIIs until Feb 1918)
No 23 Sqn, December 1917 – April 1918

United States Air Service SPAD XIII Aero Squadrons in France in 1918

1st Pursuit Group – 27th, 94th, 95th, 147th, 185th Aero Squadrons
2nd Pursuit Group – 13th, 22nd, 49th (from August 1918), 103rd (July 1918), 139th Aero Squadrons
3rd Pursuit Group – 28th, 49th (until August 1918), 93rd, 103rd (from August 1918), 213th Aero Squadrons.
4th Pursuit Group – 17th, 141st, 148th Aero Squadrons (17th and 148th transferred in from No 65 Wing RAF in October 1918 and slated to have their Camels replaced with SPAD XIIIs, but only the 141st's SPADs saw combat before the Armistice)
5th Pursuit Group – some SPAD XIIIs arrived to supplement SPAD VIIs of 138th Aero Squadron, but none saw combat before the Armistice

Italian SPAD XIII *Squadriglie* in 1917-1918

10° Gruppo – 70ª Squadriglia
17° Gruppo – 71ª, 77ª, 91ª Squadriglie

Belgian Air Force SPAD XIII *Escadrille* in 1918

10éme Escadrille, March – November 1918

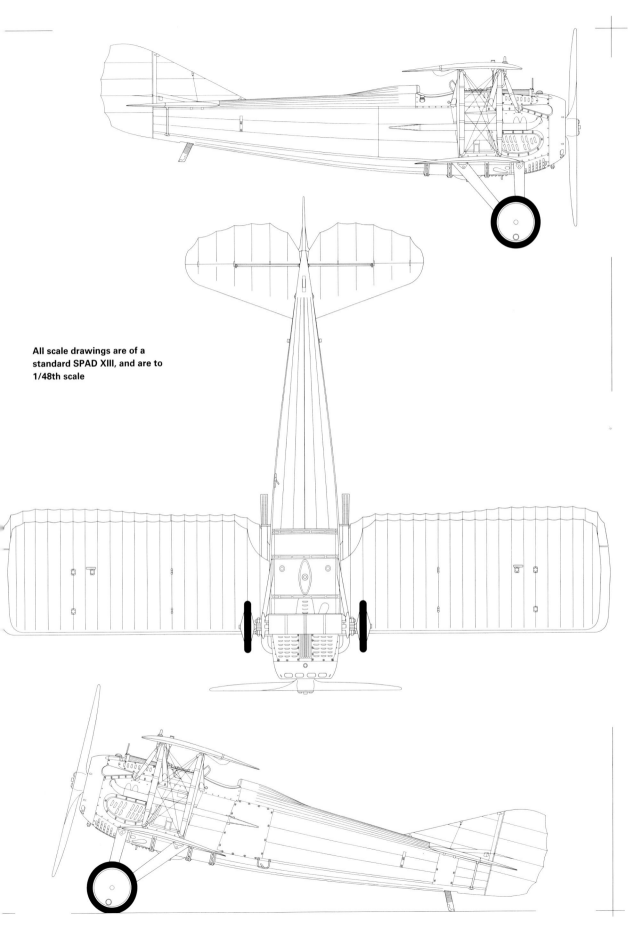

All scale drawings are of a
standard SPAD XIII, and are to
1/48th scale

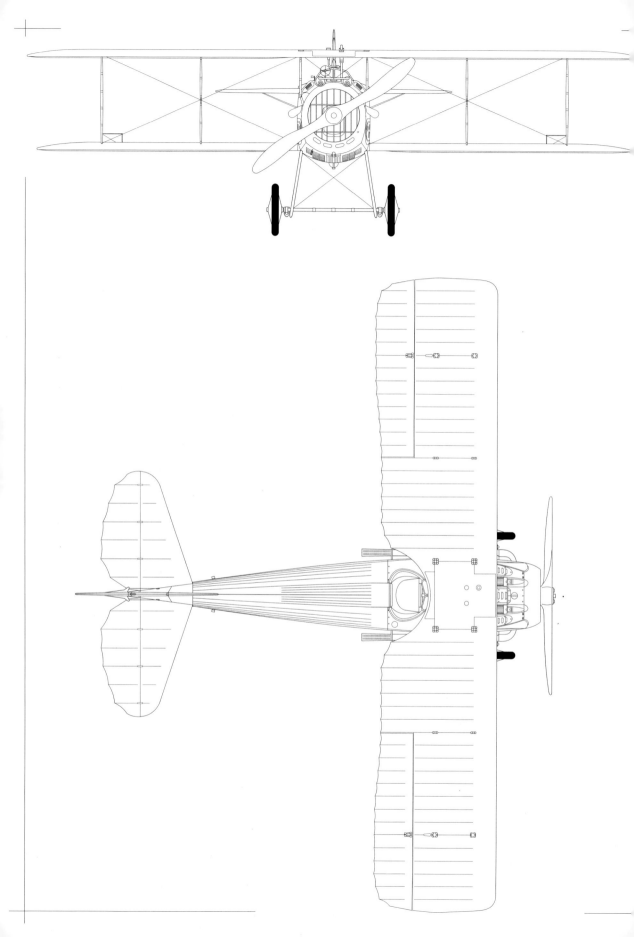

1

SPAD XII S382 of Capitaine Georges Guynemer, SPA3, July 1917

Guynemer's first SPAD XII arrived in early July 1917, and he used it to score kills on 27 and 28 July, as well as a double victory on 17 August.

2

SPAD XIII S504 of Capitaine Georges Guynemer, SPA3, September 1917

The livery of Guynemer's SPAD XIII included a black command pennant on the fuselage upper decking, an unusual variation on the tricolour band and a dark (possibly black) 'X' on the upper wing center section, the significance of which is unknown. He received S504 in late July, and used it to score his 53rd victory on 20 August 1917. Guynemer went missing in this machine on 11 September.

3

SPAD XIII (serial unknown) of Lt Benjamin Bozon-Verduraz, SPA3, May 1918

Normally flown by Bozon-Verduraz, *Mon Lion* was also used by American volunteer Sgt Frank L Baylies to claim his fifth victory on 19 May 1918.

4

SPAD XIII (serial unknown) of Lt Armand de Turenne, N12, 1918

When de Turenne took command of SPA12, he retained the emblem of his former unit. 'Personally', he wrote in a letter to the author, 'I believed that I had to keep my "Chant et Combat". After leaving SPA48, I did not have a personal number, but I always kept the cockerel'. Although de Turenne's early-model SPAD XIII lacks SPA12's blue and white pennant insignia, it features that unit's white radiator cowl.

5

SPAD XII S444 of Lt Gabriel Guérin, SPA15, Spring 1918

One of the handful of 'cannon SPADs' allotted to various *escadrilles*, S444 is believed to have been flown by Lt Gabriel Guérin who, with 23 victories, was SPA15's leading ace in the spring of 1918.

6

SPAD XIII (serial unknown) of Capitaine Joseph Marie Xavier de Sevin, SPA26, September 1918

Xavier de Sevin was already credited with six victories from his time with N12 when he was made a *Chévalier de la Légion d'Honneur* and given command of SPA26 on 25 December 1917. This may explain why he indulged in a personal motif (a rose bordered by a hunting horn), rather than the more typical number '1', to identify his SPAD XIII. De Sevin brought his wartime total to 12 on 24 October 1918.

7

SPAD XIII (serial unknown) of Lt Louis Chartoire, SPA31, July 1918

Chartoire, who was credited with five victories between

17 October 1917 and 2 November 1918, described his SPAD as wearing the number '7' and featuring red and blue quartered wheel hubs. The red and white radiator cowl was a typical supplement to SPA31's Greek archer insignia.

8

SPAD XIII (serial unknown) of Lt Georges Félix Madon, SPA38, Summer 1918

After Madon assumed command of SPA38 on 24 March 1918, his personal thistle emblem became the *escadrille* insignia. To make himself more easily identifiable to his men, he painted the fuselage and tail of his aircraft red – just as Manfred von Richthofen had done on the German side. Madon's SPAD XII, S484, and an early SPAD XIII had all-red fuselages, but at least one of his later XIIIs had a white radiator cowl as well. Madon's final tally of 41 confirmed victories – out of about 100 claims – made him the fourth-ranking French ace of World War 1.

9

SPAD XIII S10039 of Lt Charles Nungesser, SPA65, September 1918

Charles Nungesser's SAFCA-built SPAD XIII had an asymmetrical white triangle on the upper decking, which supposedly threw off the aim of an enemy pilot on his tail, as well as his familiar 'coeur noir' trademark. Also marked under the port cockpit was the name *LT VERDIER*, which was a reference to one of his best friends, Lt Louis Verdier-Fauvety, who had served in N65, then become executive officer of N124 *'Lafayette'* and finally been made CO of SPA163. He was still leading the unit when he was killed during a night bombardment on 31 August 1918. Nungesser swore to avenge him, but curiously scored no confirmed successes after his 43rd victory on 15 August 1918.

10

SPAD XIII (serial unknown) of Adjutant Pierre Gaudermen, SPA68, February-March 1918

Gaudermen, who had the number '11' applied to all his fighters, survived the war as SPA68's only ace, with five victories.

11

SPAD XIII S501 of Lt Albert Deullin, SPA73, September 1917

As one of the leading *'Stork'* aces, Deullin was among the first French pilots to receive a SPAD XIII, which Guynemer is believed to have 'borrowed', and damaged, on 10 September. S501's darker-than-usual fuselage in photographs suggests that it was refinished, as well as repaired, by the time Deullin flew it – possibly to score his 18th victory on 27 September, followed by a Pfalz D III on 8 November. Promoted to capitaine in October, Deullin was commanding GC19 when he scored his 20th and last victory on 19 May 1918.

12

SPAD XVII S694 of Lt François Battesti, SPA73, October 1918

GC12 received a small number of new SPAD XVIIs in the last

weeks of the war, and this particular example was issued to the unit's Corsican-born seven-victory ace, Lt François Battesti, who served with SPA73. There is no surviving record to indicate whether any of the SPAD XVIIs that reached squadron service actually saw any combat.

13
SPAD XIII S2287 of Lt Robert Delannoy, SPA80, Spring 1918
Blériot-built SPAD XIII S2287 came to grief after engine trouble compelled Lt Robert Delannoy to land, after which he said, 'My aeroplane ran into a power line. It lost speed and fell on its wing'. Already an ace with five victories from 1917, Delannoy was flying a SPAD XIII when he was credited with destroying a Halberstadt CL II and an unidentified enemy two-seater on 20 August 1918.

14
SPAD XIII (serial unknown) of 1Lt G DeFreest Larner, SPA86, March 1918
'I deliberately chose the number "13" for all my SPADs', said G DeFreest Larner, 'just as I always lighted three cigarettes on a match when I could – just for the devilment. As I recall, whilst I was with *Escadrille* SPA86 all my aeroplanes were uncamouflaged, but had the wing and star insignia of SPA86 painted in red on the fuselage sides'. Larner scored two victories with SPA86 and later flew Blériot-built SPAD XIII S2742, still marked with '13', while leading 'B Flight' of the 103rd Aero Squadron. He added five more kills to his tally with this squadron.

15
SPAD XIII (serial unknown) of Sous-Lt Marcel Coadou, SPA88, November 1918
According to Coadou, his SPAD XIIIs bore the horizontal yellow-black-yellow bands of SPA88 on the fuselage sides and radiator cowl, as well as diagonal bands on the upper wing. In addition to the number '4', he used blue as a personal marking on the vertical stabiliser, wheel hubs and the upper surfaces of the ailerons and elevators. Coadou's nickname 'Judex' appeared under the right side of the cockpit only, and he added iron crosses to the white of his tricolour fuselage band for each German aeroplane he claimed – a total of nine by the end of the war.

16
SPAD XII (serial unknown) of Lt Marcel Hugues, SPA95, May 1918
Lt Marcel Anatole Hugues, who had ten victories to his credit when he took command of SPA95 on 7 March 1918, is known to have flown a SPAD XII in May. He seems to have person-alised this machine by applying the unit insignia to the fuselage upper decking in place of a commander's pennant. Hugues downed an enemy aeroplane over Mesnil St Georges on 11 April 1918, and scored his 12th and last victory in concert with Sgt Jules Fleury on 3 May, although it is not certain whether he used his 'Cannon SPAD' on either occasion.

17
SPAD XII S445 of Sous-Lt René Fonck, SPA103, May 1918
Fonck downed his first enemy aeroplane in a SPAD XII on 19 May 1918, and went on to claim ten more victories, of which seven were confirmed, while flying the 'Cannon SPAD'.

18
SPAD XIII (serial unknown) of Capitaine René Fonck, SPA103, Autumn 1918
Fonck is known to have flown at least two different SPAD XIIIs, one bearing the Roman numeral 'VI' in red, outlined in white, and another similarly marked with the numeral IX. Fonck's total score of 75 confirmed victories – out of 127 claims – made him the leading Allied ace of World War 1.

19
SPAD XII (serial unknown) of Sgts Fernand Chavannes and Lionel de Marmier, SPA112, Summer 1918
As the highest-scoring pilots in SPA112, and being close friends, Chavannes and de Marmier 'shared' the only SPAD XII allotted to their *escadrille*, as signifed by their intertwined initials on the fuselage sides.

20
SPAD XIII (serial unknown) of Sgt Fernand Chavannes, SPA112, August 1918
SPA112 aircraft featured two red fuselage bands and personal motifs of the pilots' choice. Chavannes' Adolphe Bernard-built SPAD XIII may have been the most extravagant, with a black spider web over part of the fuselage, on which a white spider – with a French cockade on its head – pursued a 'German' fly with Maltese crosses on its wings! Chavannes survived the war with seven victories.

21
SPAD XIII (serial unknown) of Lt Leon Jean-Pierre Bourjade, SPA152, Summer 1918
Jean-Pierre Bourjade, who was studying to be a Catholic missionary when the war broke out, was photographed in a SPAD XIII bearing the number '13', apparently in yellow, as well as the crocodile insignia of SPA152. Another Blériot-built SPAD that he flew was more personally decorated, with a white band, a headrest partially painted red, a portrait of his patron, Sainte Thérèse, and a pennant of the Sacré-Coeur flying after of the cockpit. Bourjade was the war's most successful balloon specialist with 27 destroyed – he also downed a solitary German fighter.

22
SPAD XIII S4472 of Capitaine Pavel Argeyev, SPA124, June 1918
All of Argeyev's SPADs during his time with SPA124 bore the number '19', including S4472, which was eventually adorned with a bust of Joan of Arc on the diagonal white band that served as the *escadrille* insignia. After scoring his first six victories in Russia, Argeyev added nine more with SPA124 to become its second-raking ace after another foreign volunteer in the *escadrille's* ranks, American G Raoul Lufbery.

23
SPAD XIII S8313(?) of Sous-Lt Robert Yvon Paul Waddington, SPA154, Summer 1918
Individual markings in SPA154 were generally limited to serial numbers, although a few pilots added names under the cock-

pit. An exception was Sgt Wainwright Abbott's Blériot-built aeroplane, on which he defiantly added the 'unlucky' number '13' to the red fuselage band that served as the unit marking. After Abbott left SPA154, Robert Waddington flew it for the same reason. Ten of Waddington's twelve victories – including five balloons – were scored with SPA154.

24

SPAD XIII S4830 of Lt Michel Joseph Callixte Marie Coiffard, SPA154, October 1918

Wainwright Abbott stated that in September 1918, SPA154 replaced its red band with a stylised black-and-white crane, 'a migratory bird with powerful wings', applied over a light blue patch on the fuselage side. This marking was almost certainly worn by the Blériot-built SPAD S15060 of Adjutant Paul Petit and the Adolphe Bernard-built SPAD S7921 of Adjutant Jacques Ehrlich when they downed a balloon on 18 September – and were then pounced on by a patrol of Fokker D VIIs, Petit being killed and Ehrlich being forced down and capured. Coiffard's last SPAD, a Levasseur-built machine, had an unpainted radiator cowl, red wheel hubs and *Valentine*, the name of the woman he planned to marry in November, painted beneath the cockpit. Tragically, Coiffard was mortally wounded during a fight with Fokker D VIIs on 28 October 1918, by which time he had destroyed 26 balloons and eight aeroplanes.

25

SPAD XIII (serial unknown) of Capitaine Henri Hay de Slade, SPA159, Autumn 1918

'I did not know how to impart my techniques to others', Slade commented when asked about being made CO of the demoralized SPA159 on 29 July 1918, 'so I had my SPAD XIII painted all over with prominent red stripes down the fuselage, and before taking the men up on patrol I told them that in the event of combat, to stay up and watch what I did – the red stripes should have made it easy enough to recognise me in the most confused dogfight'. Leading by example, Slade succeeded in improving SPA159's performance, and by the end of the war, the unit had downed 12 enemy aeroplanes, eight of which were credited to Slade, which boosted his final total to 19.

26

SPAD XIII S4764 of Sgt André Lévy, SPA561, September 1918

SPA561's only ace in Italy, Sgt André Robert Lévy was flying Levasseur-built SPAD XIII S4764 on 16 September 1918 when he flamed a balloon for his sixth victory, only to be brought down by Austro-Hungarian anti-aircraft fire and taken prisoner. After two attempts, he managed to escape on 4 November.

27

SPAD XIII B.6847 of Capt William M Fry, No 23 Sqn, January 1918

A veteran with previous experience in Morane-Saulnier and Nieuport fighters prior to joining No 23 Sqn, Willy Fry was flying SPAD XIII B.6847 when he downed an Albatros in flames over Houthulst Forest on 23 January 1918. He scored his 11th and final victory in a Sopwith Dolphin of No 79 Sqn

on 11 May 1918. Meanwhile, Canadian Lt John Finlay Noel MacRae used B.6847 to down a Rumpler two-seater on 9 March, later raising his total to five.

28

SPAD XIII B'6846 of Capts H F S Drewitt and James Fitz-Morris, No 23 Sqn, March 1918

Capt James Fitz-Morris was flying B'6846 when he shot down a Rumpler two-seater over Urvillers on 7 March 1918, then teamed up with Lts J F N MacRae and G W R Pidsley to down a second Rumpler south of Masniéres two days later. New Zealander Capt Herbert Frank Stacey Drewitt used B'6846 to down a two-seater on 11 March 1918 for his fourth victory of an eventual tally of seven.

29

SPAD XIII (serial unknown) of Maggiore Francesco Baracca, *91ª Squadriglia*, Spring 1918

The best known of the many aircraft to bear Baracca's famous 'cavallino rampante' emblem was an early Blériot-built SPAD XIII, which also had red squadron leader's pennants attached to the inner set of interplane struts. Baracca's tally of 34 victories before his death on 19 June 1918 made him Italy's 'ace of aces'.

30

SPAD XIII (serial unknown) of Capitano Bartolomeo Constantini, *91ª Squadriglia*, August 1918

Constantini's early Blériot-built SPAD XIII displays both the griffon adopted by *91ª Squadriglia* as a unit insignia and Roman numerals for individual identification. After scoring his first four victories in SPAD VIIs in 1917, 'Bortolo' Constantini used the SPAD XIII to down an Albatros D III on 12 August 1918 and to send a two-seater down in flames over Marano di Piave on 22 August – he reported seeing the observer parachute to safety from his latter victim.

31

SPAD XIII S4489 of Capt Charles J Biddle, 13th Aero Squadron, October 1918

Kellner-built SPAD XIII S4489 was assigned to the 13th Aero Squadron on 7 July 1918, and was returned to French control on 15 December. Biddle's personal livery included a blue and white radiator cowl – probably in memory of his earlier French unit, SPA73 – and a commander's tricolour band. In addition, there were victory marks in the form of five notches in the 'Grim Reaper's' bloody scythe, and four tiny crosses behind the running skeleton. Another cross above the tricolour band represented a patched bullet hole.

32

SPAD XIII (serial unknown) of 1Lt William Howard Stovall, 13th Aero Squadron, November 1918

In the war's final weeks, six-victory ace 'Hank' Stovall decorated his SPAD with white and red stripes and white diamonds, in addition to the normal squadron livery. During World War 2, Stovall rose in rank to chief of staff to Gen Carl Spaatz, who had flown alongside him in the 13th Aero Squadron in September 1918. Retiring as a colonel, he returned to the cotton business at the Stovall plantation in Mississippi, where he died on 11 May 1970.